LEMONA

Predictable Profits from Refreshingly Simple Systems - The Small Business Sales and Marketing Guide

Gareth Everson

Your First Step

Scan the QR code to **meet HeyPip**, your own systems-savvy AI assistant who helps you **put these systems to work** in **AI-fast time** - so you can enjoy even **more profitable growth**, right now

lemonadeplan.com/step1

Second edition

ISBN: 9781068387401

In memory of 'Big Len' Berry, a man sparing with words but generous in actions, who didn't turn me into an engineer like those before me but did show this 'button pusher' that concrete results come from mixing one part clear thinking, two parts resilience, and four parts focused effort.

Acknowledgments

With thanks to Allan Simmons (foreword), Alexander Valchev (cover design), Col Gray (artwork), Adrian Wilson (photography), James Ashford, Nico Ceballos Jones and Peter Thomson (positioning and launch), Wayne Alexander, Peter Daly-Dickson, Rob Drummond, Susan Heaton-Wright, Alasdair McWilliam, Katie Spreadbury and Jeroen Vos (proofreaders)

Contents

Diagrams

Foreword

"When I first met Gareth, I was a business owner doing okay but frustrated and running myself ragged. I hadn't gone into business to chase my tail or to work too many hours to be healthy. I knew I could do better; it shouldn't be this hard.

Countless 'gurus' had told me I needed to systemise everything and do this or that marketing 'thing', which felt confusing and disjointed. I was standing too close to see that I had tangled myself up working 'in' the business with a spaghetti of partial and disjointed processes. What I was missing is what you now hold in your hand – a proven framework that brings together sales, marketing and operational strategies and systems that, until now, are usually only taught separately, not as an integrated framework.

"Begin with the end in mind," which you'll see referred to in the book, resonated immediately in my first discussions with Gareth. That was back in 2015. I had searched for someone to help make my carpet cleaning business run more smoothly and profitably. I didn't want someone to run those systems for me. I needed someone who could identify what was working, pinpoint missing opportunities, and provide practical strategies to take my business to the next level in a way that made me feel in control. Gareth proved to be that person.

Within months, the impact was incredible. My carpet cleaning business became more profitable, with complete systems from start to finish. This gave me time to work on my other venture: a software business for the carpet cleaning industry, which Gareth has also helped me grow.

His unique ability to help business owners take charge of their operations sets Gareth apart. He understands systems and offers straightforward, actionable suggestions based on this methodology. His insights showed me how to implement solutions that created a golden triangle of improved efficiency, even higher client satisfaction, and helped free up my time to work more 'on' my businesses.

Over time, as I watched Gareth help many other business owners across various industries, I saw that his approach worked for more than just me. It worked well for almost everyone, including businesses with limited prior sales and marketing experience. He'd begun referring to his business framework as **LEMONADE Plan**, a neat metaphor for putting the zest back into systems and marketing processes. It's a name that captures the revitalising impact on service businesses. **LEMONADE**'s steps work like enablers rather than ones that overwhelm – from building predictable numbers of leads to turning clients into raving fans and generating reviews and referrals that drive growth.

This book is an invaluable guide if you want clarity and predictability in your business and want to enjoy profitable growth. Gareth's insights will help you take action and feel in control, and I'm confident you'll find the same value in his methodology as I have. It's an honour to share my recommendation for Gareth and the **LEMONADE Plan**."

Allan Simmons

Clean and Dry Carpet, Rug, Upholstery and Stone Cleaning

and GetBookedUp Software

Preface:
Are You at a Fork in the Road?

Being a small business owner in the twenty-first century has felt like being inside a washing machine on a relentless spin cycle, getting faster with each spin. As one cycle started, the next rapidly followed: high-speed internet, social media, economic crises, a global pandemic, and the rise of AI. Each rewriting how business works faster than before.

Consumers have become less tolerant, more opinionated, and have shorter attention spans than ever. If a digital interaction doesn't deliver, the next one is available at the next scroll. And if you think digital is brutal, take a moment to reflect on the direction of travel for *personal* interactions: they're rapidly changing towards the 'wholly ignored' too.

Every 'new normal' of business has been shaped by the twists and turns of every 'new normal' that came before it. Each created opportunities for more business startups, and – simultaneously – the constant churn explains why just 39% of them survive five years or longer (ONS). Worse, just 1 in 10 self-employed business owners earns more than £5,000 per month (IFS Study), and the average owner spends a mere 46% of their working time on actual client work (Xero study). It's like getting a job and discovering you'll only be paid from Wednesday afternoons to Fridays.

I've spent fifteen years working with small businesses, and every week, I meet brilliant experts in their fields trapped in these feast-to-famine sales cycles. Despite having more technology than ever to help them, they're exhausted, sometimes *because* of technology's role. Their authenticity struggles to be heard above the digital noise, fighting for attention in an increasingly crowded space.

All around them, these owners see others achieving consistent growth while their hard work fails to deliver the same rewards. They, perhaps like you?, feel like they just about keep the business wheels turning thanks to the demand for their skills and professional expertise. But many have had to get comfortable in discomfort – low profits, their ambition withered, their energy expired, too committed to the business to return to employment, but too many plates spinning to get clarity about improving it. It's business **stagnation**, if not yet business **failure**.

Think about that. Stagnation. The slow death of dreams, the gradual acceptance of mediocrity, the quiet resignation to "this is just how it is."

And yet, some businesses aren't just surviving, they're thriving.

They found something that works regardless of market turbulence. They thrive with consistent profits and glowing client reviews, often without a background in sales or marketing. Many of my clients have sold their companies for strong revenue multiples, built sustainable wealth for retirement, or achieved consistent growth by mastering systematic delivery and prioritising customer service and value. These aren't just isolated success stories or lucky breaks.

Four years ago, I started studying what successful businesses do differently that others don't or won't. I was frustrated that most business books and marketing training fall back on unachievable 'must-dos' or expect you to be a sales or marketing expert. But the point is that **most of us don't start with those skills**, do we? So, the challenge shifted to recompiling years of my real-world experiences, conversations, notes, and tests in a simple-to-follow way that became this book.

You'll discover multiple foundational pillars. One of these foundations, in particular, could be why your past attempts to improve your processes failed: they need a **step-by-step implementation order**. You just started with the wrong processes first. The order matters. Those who succeed because they're already good at sales or marketing often overlook this when they try to tell you how to fix your business systems. It makes their advice focus too much on the skill that got them there. However, over 95% of UK businesses have fewer than 10 employees, and 77% are one-person businesses. You can only do so much. Most business owners aren't experts at sales or marketing. They can't fix everything at once, especially the most challenging processes. It leads to false starts, which is why most companies fail with systems.

But **the right processes, in the right order, the right way** create effervescent energy. Leads become more consistent. Sales conversations flow naturally. Delivery becomes systematic. Reviews and referrals accelerate the cycle. Most importantly, you regain control of your time, growth, and future.

I call this business framework 'LEMONADE'.

LEMONADE Plan is the best way to make your eight key business processes fizz[1]. As you read this book, you'll learn 'how' to create the structure to launch the processes your business needs and, importantly, the 'order' in which to launch them and why that matters.

You're standing at a fork in the road.

In one direction, garish neon signs advertise the latest marketing hack or gizmo. But shortly afterwards, the road suddenly stops, and signs divert you back, and you recall you've been here before, multiple times. Those neon signs change every few months, but it's the same road to mediocrity, and it's paved with burned-out business owners.

The other direction is towards systems and repeatable processes. This road leads to clarity, consistency, and growth and helps you build wealth and a business that someone else would want to buy.

Don't choose the wrong direction. I've been there. One of my early business ventures failed. It was costly, exhausting, and embarrassing. However, it taught me lessons I've used when I've struggled since then and helped me prevent other business owners from making the same mistakes.

I wrote this book to help business owners achieve their dreams instead of giving up on them. I'm tired of watching brilliant people settle for less than they deserve. It's saddening to see capable owners sacrifice their health, relationships, and dreams because they can't step away

---

1 For non-British readers, British lemonade is ***not*** the still, homemade, sun-soaked drink of first entrepreneurial ventures that you might be picturing. It's a clear, fizzy and highly carbonated drink like Sprite.

from daily firefighting or doing ever more for lower returns.

This framework isn't about temporary fixes or trendy shortcuts. It's about doing things the right way, in the correct order. It will give you proven processes to make things better than the constant chaos most owners endure and transform your business from scattered tactics to systematic growth.

You'll meet four business owners, Sarah, James, Michael and Emma, and see how they discovered and implemented these principles. Their stories might feel familiar. I'll keep adding my thoughts on their situation throughout the book in grey boxes like this one, making them easy to jump to.

There's also a fifth business owner; the most important one: **you**. I've developed an AI assistant called **HeyPip** who'll help you put these systems to work in AI-fast time. As you read LEMONADE Plan, chat with HeyPip to put the same steps into your own strategy. Start here with the QR code:

Have You Taken The First Step?

Scan the QR code to **meet HeyPip**, your own systems-savvy AI assistant who helps you **put these systems to work** in **AI-fast time** - so you can enjoy even **more profitable growth**, right now

lemonadeplan.com/step1

Let's put some systematic zest in your business.

Gareth Everson

Got questions? Email: garetheverson@heypip.ai

Part 1: The End Goal

Chapter 1: Begin With the End in Mind

"Begin with the end in mind. Start with the final product and work backwards to the starting point."

- Stephen Covey, author of 'The 7 Habits of Highly Effective People'

Scene: with Sarah, the business coach, in her office

Sarah stared at her laptop screen, the numbers blurring as tears threatened. It was another month of silence, another dip in the rollercoaster. Her business account balance, healthy for a few months after three new client signings, had dwindled quickly. In February, her LinkedIn posts had landed perfectly, bringing five sales calls and three clients. That validation felt amazing, proof that she could help other businesses grow.

But now? Nothing. No calls, no emails, no interest. In the busyness of delivering those client projects, she'd completely dropped the ball on generating new leads. Worse, she'd forgotten to ask those happy clients for reviews. Even her most successful client, who'd more than doubled their revenue using her guidance, remained a silent success story: no testimonials, case studies, or referrals – nothing to show future clients what was possible.

Sarah opened Google and searched 'business coach near me'. Her competitors' profiles sat on top, gleaming with five-star reviews and glowing testimonials even though they had less client experience than her. Each one tells a story of transformation, each review brings them more visibility, and each success builds their reputation. Meanwhile, her business stayed buried further down the listings. She hadn't shared her client successes and wasn't showing her expertise to the people who needed it most.

Here she was again: contrary to those client successes, she was having another day where she felt like a fraud and an imposter as a business owner. Sarah was in the feast-or-famine cycle again, and that same dark thought was back: "Maybe I'm not cut out for running this as my own business."

At 47, with two teenagers heading towards university and a mortgage that wouldn't pay itself, she couldn't keep riding this revenue rollercoaster. Something had to change. She was brilliant at helping other businesses build structures to grow, so why did her success feel so random?

The Two Markers of Success

With so many ways to measure success, it's easy to lose sight of what matters. If you take nothing else away from this book, get clarity on this: just two clear markers separate thriving businesses from those merely surviving:

1. **Profit** is the first function of your business. It measures whether your past actions have yielded a return: you marketed, priced, sold, and delivered something that gave your customers value, making enough money to keep your business healthy. Profit is not – on its own – a predictor of future success but is a 'lagging indicator' of past success.

2. **Systematic Endorsements** show that your work is making a difference in people's lives, and they are happy to tell others via public reviews, referrals or case studies about you. People don't refer businesses, they refer experiences. Endorsements are the 'leading indicator' of future success: the momentum created by recent reviews or referrals will likely lead to future success.

If you're getting regular and consistent **endorsements** in a systemised way, you know that you'll be in a position going forward where **profit** becomes more predictable and attainable. But one without the other probably means your success will only be temporary.

Think of these markers like the bubbles in a glass of lemonade (or 'soda' if you're reading this in a country where lemonade is not carbonated). When the business systems that sustain them work correctly, the markers rise consistently and create sustainable growth. When your systems are random or broken, everything eventually goes flat.

Sarah's story shows what happens when these markers, and the systems that sustain them, are missing, at least in part. Her expertise helped other businesses grow, yet her profits remained unpredictable. Her clients valued her, yet she had no systematic way to turn client success into visible endorsements. Each piece of her business, from lead generation to review collection, ran on sporadic bursts of energy rather than reliable systems to connect them.

These aren't just nice-to-haves. They're the essential ingredients of sustainable growth. *Predictable profits* come when you have systemised processes behind how you **attract**, **sell** to, **onboard** and **delight** your clients (or customers, guests or patients – I'll use the terms interchangeably in this book). *Systematic endorsements* come when you deliberately design processes that make reviews, referrals, and repeat sales natural outcomes from those processes that come before, not happy accidents.

Most importantly, these markers form a virtuous cycle. Systematic endorsements fuel lead generation, making profit generation more predictable. Meanwhile, predictable profits provide the resources and stability to deliver experiences worthy of endorsement. When one marker strengthens, it naturally reinforces the other.

Fig 1.1: ***The Profits & Endorsements Success Loop***

The Success Loop is the core of how you measure success in your business. Predictable profits and systematic endorsements create continuous business growth. Each feeds into and strengthens the other, enabling small businesses to break free from random marketing efforts and build sustainable, scalable success.

Why most businesses never achieve either

The traditional approach to business growth resembles Sarah's early efforts, working harder rather than systematically. You post on social media when inspiration strikes, follow up with leads when you remember, and ask for reviews when you think of it. You only tackle each task when you have energy and time, creating feast-or-famine cycles that keep you in survival mode.

Most businesses run out of time and resources before they exhaust their market's potential. Worse, most business owners exhaust their energy before they run out of opportunities. This happens because:

- Limited capacity leads to reactive decisions rather than strategic growth
- You spend most of your time on immediate survival tasks
- You market randomly instead of systematically
- The cost of acquiring each new client stays unnecessarily high
- Energy goes to firefighting instead of building sustainable systems

Consider this: at any one time, only 2% of all the people who could buy from you are actively engaged and looking to buy. The remaining 98% represents untapped potential. This considerable opportunity exists not because the market doesn't have the problems you solve but because most businesses lack the systems to efficiently capture, educate and convert people who might buy from you in the future.

Fig 1.2: ***The Old Way vs. The Systematic Way to do Business***

This shows the key differences between the random, unplanned 'old' ways of doing business and the structured, 'systematic' way. The left side shows the pitfalls of ad hoc marketing, while the right side shows the benefits of a more systematic approach. Standardising and automating processes (centre) are transition points to achieving stable, scalable results.

Choose your version of "hard"

Every business owner faces a simple but profound choice. You can:

1. work hard until you burn out at random activities, never knowing what results you'll get or;
2. work hard in the short term to build systems that deliver predictable outcomes

Both paths require effort. The difference is that one builds sustainable, ongoing success, while the other keeps you strapped into a revenue rollercoaster. Each time your business goes up and down, it gets scarier until you just want it to stop. Systems beat individual effort every time.

Just as Sarah discovered, expertise alone isn't enough. She'd been running towards personal and business burnout when she needed the energy boost from more predictable profits and endorsements that more joined-up systems and processes would deliver.

Who this book is for

This book is for service-based business owners who:

- Have multiple customers, clients, patients or guests each month
- Know that with better, longer-term follow-up, they could make more sales
- Could be making more money if they could just get their systems and processes in order
- Trust their expertise but struggle with marketing and systems
- Rely on word-of-mouth, but know they're missing

opportunities

Businesses like, but not limited to:

- Business services providers (like coaches, consultants, accountants, trainers, freelancers)
- Health and wellness providers (like physiotherapists and personal trainers)
- Home services providers (like trades, installers, and cleaning services)
- Leisure and accommodation providers (B&Bs, experiences, private health clubs)

Most importantly, this book is for business owners ready to transform random success into systematic growth. You're in the right place if you're tired of the feast-or-famine cycle and prepared to build something more predictable.

How successful businesses think differently

Sarah's phone buzzed, a WhatsApp message from Emma, the VA member in her networking group: "Sorry, can't make today's networking meetup. Promised the kids we'd go for ice creams after school. Got all my client work done today."

Sarah felt a familiar mix of admiration and envy. While she rode the feast-or-famine rollercoaster, Emma's VA business seemed consistently profitable. There were no gaps between clients, steady monthly income, and somehow still time for family. Last week, over coffee, Emma mentioned she hadn't actively looked for a new client in months.

"How do you stay so booked up?" Sarah typed back.

"Funny thing," Emma replied, "I used to chase every opportunity going. Now, I just focus on doing great work that gets talked about. My marketing pretty much runs itself off the back of the reviews."

Sarah typed 'Perfect Review' at the top of her notes. If this had brought Emma consistent success without the firefighting, maybe Sarah needed to work backwards from there, start with the end in mind and build systems to make those glowing testimonials inevitable. This document was about to change everything for Sarah. Instead of trying to fix her marketing first, she was beginning with the end goal, those glowing testimonials that would bring her predictable leads, referrals, and revenue.

This 'working backwards' approach transforms how you build your business:

- Start with your desired endorsements – what do you want clients to say and do when you've completed your first piece of work with them?
- Design delivery systems that consistently create those experiences
- Build service packages your systems can reliably fulfil
- Create natural add-on opportunities that make sense
- Focus lead generation on finding the kinds of clients that are a great fit for your offer and delivery model
- Educate prospects about your systematic approach
- Convert qualified leads through structured conversations
- Onboard new clients in ways that maintain momentum

Think of it like planning a journey. Most businesses start by trying different lead generation tactics, hoping they'll eventually reach their destination. Working backwards is different. You begin by defining precisely where you want to end up (those perfect reviews and predictable profits), then build the systematic path to get there.

WORKING BACKWARDS FRAMEWORK

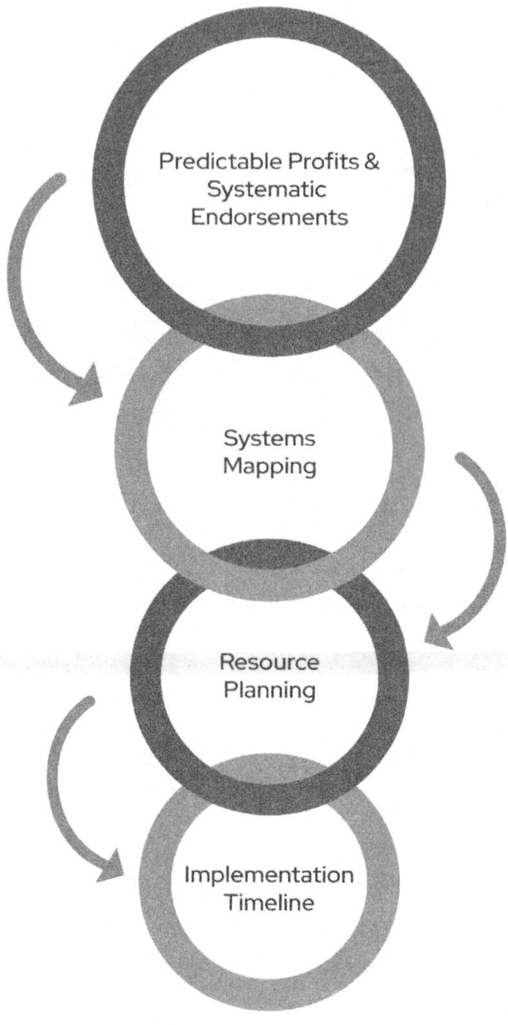

Fig 1.3: ***The Working Backwards Framework***

This shows the process where you start with clear profit and endorsements goals and then work backwards to plan the necessary steps to achieve them. It shows the three key stages: Systems Mapping, Resource Planning, and Implementation. When you start with your target outcomes and work backwards you have a path to success that makes sure each stage aligns with your final objective.

It takes careful thought and implementation to transform random business activities into predictable, systemised success. But consider the alternative: continuing with scattered efforts that drain your energy without creating sustainable results. This book breaks down that transformation into manageable pieces and shows you how to build systematic success one process at a time.

Think of it like renovating a house. You wouldn't try to remodel every room simultaneously. Instead, you'd work methodically, ensuring each improvement fits well in a more functional home. Your business transformation deserves the same careful attention. You'll take the one-project-at-a-time approach as budget and time allow. Many will be DIY projects; others might require outside help. So, prioritise carefully and decide which projects bring the most value to you.

Questions to consider

Scan the QR code to chat with HeyPip AI to get clarity and a tailored plan on this topic in your business. lemonadeplan.com/ch1

In every chapter, I'll ask you to think about how the topic relates to your business. You can interact via chat with **HeyPip**, the AI marketing assistant, trained on this book and the best marketing knowledge on the internet.

If you're more 'pen and paper', download a printable version of the end of chapter questions at lemonadeplan.com/resources. Alternatively, grab a pen or highlighter and doodle in the book.

In Chapter 2, we'll explore how systems beat tactics every time. But before we do so, take a moment to reflect on the following:

1. Look at your last five client reviews or testimonials. What kind of words or phrases would you love future clients to say about you?

2. What would they need to experience in your service to say that?

3. Think about times you have feast-or-famine cycles. Where do opportunities slip through the cracks because your marketing or sales are inconsistent or random?

Remember: Just as lemonade loses its fizz if left unattended, random business activities can't create sustainable success. It's time to add some systematic sparkle to your approach.

Sarah wasn't alone in her journey from scattered systems to systematic success. Other business owners in her local networking group faced similar challenges:

- James, a heating engineer, was overwhelmed by quotes and admin.
- Michael, a physiotherapist, was struggling to nurture potential patients.
- Emma, a virtual assistant, had systems that required the same attention she gave her clients' businesses.

Each would find their own path through systems, and their stories offer unique process improvement insights that could help you in your service business. Let's check in on James and how he discovered that systems beat individual effort every time.

Chapter 2: The Power of Systems

"A bad system will beat a good person every time."

- W. Edwards Deming, a quality management principles pioneer who transformed manufacturing, particularly in post-war Japan

Scene: with James, a heating engineer, at the Thompsons' house

James knelt beside young Max, sitting wrapped in his duvet, watching cartoons. "Feel that?" James asked, holding his hand near the radiator. It's getting warmer already, isn't it?" The boy nodded, a sleepy smile replacing the shivers from earlier. James had arrived at breakfast time, and as another day ended well into the evening, the new combi-boiler hummed efficiently in the utility room, and another installation was finally finished.

"You're a lifesaver," Susie Thompson said, bouncing her toddler on her hip. "None of the other boiler installers I messaged could come for days. We couldn't face another cold night with just electric heaters."

He should have felt good about the praise. Instead, James's stomach tightened as his phone buzzed again. It was the busiest time of year for boiler repairs, and this buzz was the fourth customer quote request today. His diary was already packed for three weeks, and Tom (his only employee) was booked solid, too.

Today's squeezed-in job would mean another evening at his laptop, overwhelmed with paperwork. Two more quotes from last week still weren't done, Monday's invoices remained unsent, and his inbox overflowed with urgent requests.

James' business card would join the others in the Thompsons' kitchen drawer, waiting for the next heating emergency. Meanwhile, those competitors at the top of the local search results chose the best jobs from their customer requests for the more valuable, planned installations James preferred. The irony felt like a kick in the gut. He could solve almost any heating system problem but couldn't fix his business operations, which frustrated him every week.

He'd taken on Tom six months ago with a plan to free up time for growth. Instead, James found himself trapped, expert engineer by day, overwhelmed administrator by night. The extra engineer meant they could take on more work, but with it came more sales, marketing, and operations admin to keep things running. That dream of a third or fourth engineer? It felt further away with each quote request, pulling him back to his laptop instead of moving his business forward.

Why Systems Beat Tactics

James walked through the Thompsons' kitchen, his tools packed away. His expertise made him exceptional at his trade but trapped him. Like most technical experts, he'd spent years mastering his trade, learning diagnostics, and performing quality projects. His attention to detail earned glowing praise from clients like the Thompsons. Being too focused on perfection was stopping his business from growing.

He could clearly see what was going wrong:

- Every quote needed his involvement
- Each customer communication consumed evening hours
- He forgot to follow up with clients during busy periods
- Cash flow dried up because invoicing got delayed
- He only did marketing when he remembered (translation: 'if at all')
- Even having a second engineer meant double the admin but no more time

The problem wasn't a lack of skill or demand. It was the absence of systems that could scale beyond individual effort. James could handle being responsible for making the sales or being one of the engineers, but trying to do both meant doing neither as well as he wanted to.

James' phone rang. It was Michael, his physiotherapist friend. "Are you coming to 5-a-side this week?"

"Sorry, mate." James sighed. "Drowning in quotes. Seem to spend every evening catching up on admin."

"How's that then?" Michael replied. "Our businesses are pretty similar. We both fix broken things. When I start with a new patient, I explain their care pathway on one simple page. That doesn't involve explaining every stretch and exercise they need."

"Ha, sounds easy, Mike. So you're not missing 5-a-side then?"

"Nope, definitely not. Look, got to run. But look at it this way: your customers need to understand their heating solution, not every pipe fitting. So why bury yourself and them in quote details that just lead to more questions?"

James looked at his to-do list. Friday's quotes were still waiting. Michael had a point. It wasn't like his patients were being left with sticking plasters on stiff knees. Having a proper process for this would beat his current chaos.

What if they generated quotes using a process that anyone could follow? What if follow-ups happened automatically, and reviews were collected without James having to remember? This is where systems beat individual effort every time.

A systematic approach meant:

- Having fixed prices for typical jobs would help him write quotes faster and make them more consistent
- Automated follow-ups would keep customers informed and engaged
- Review requests could trigger at the perfect moment
- Simple processes that new team members could follow
- Freedom to focus on business growth rather than daily firefighting

This wasn't about reducing quality but finding ways to do great work every time.

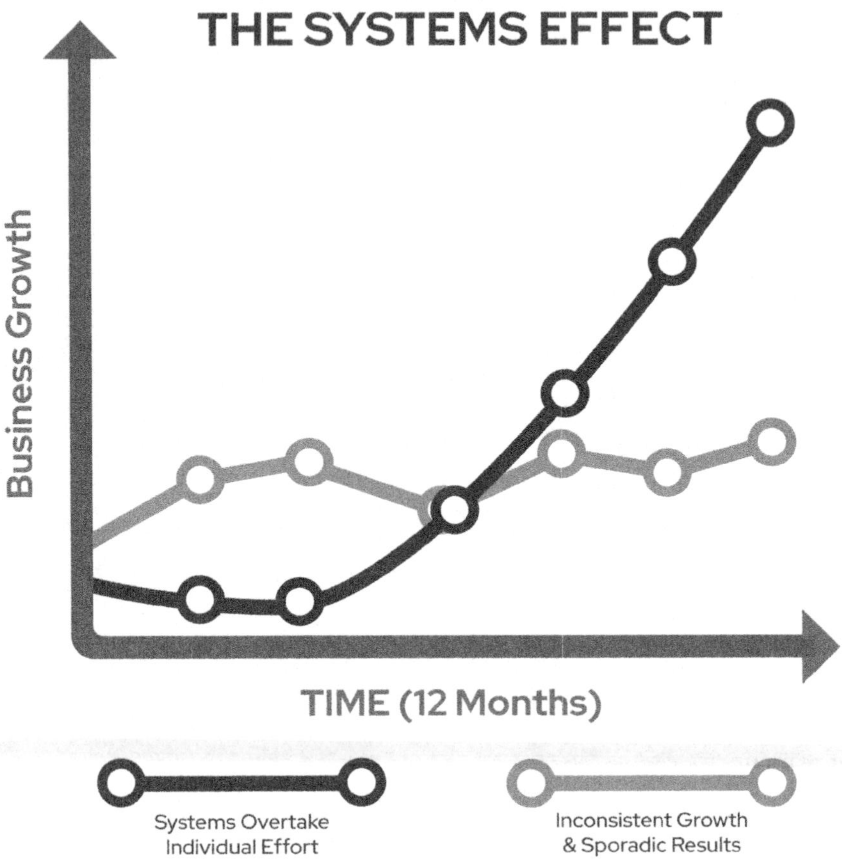

Fig 2.1: ***The Systems Effect Graph***

The graph shows the business growth trajectories of systematic versus ad hoc approaches to business operations over a 12 month timeframe. The dark line shows the steady, consistent growth achieved through systems; the lighter line shows the sporadic and inconsistent results of ad hoc efforts. It shows where the cumulative effect of systems overtakes individual, unstructured work.

The Ripple Effect of Reviews

Back home, James realised he'd forgotten to ask the Thompsons for a review. Their five-star rating could have helped future customers choose his company over competitors. Their story – from shivering child to cosy home – would have been perfect for showing what his company could do. But, like most reviews, he would lose the opportunity to ask for it in tomorrow's rush of emergency calls. Even when he remembered to ask for them, one-off reviews didn't create sustainable growth. A systematic collection of reviews would.

When he looked at his and his competitors' listings on Google Maps, James could see how consistent reviews create benefits that get bigger over time:

- Positive reviews build trust with emergency callout customers who need quick decisions
- Reviews mentioning specific boiler brands and services boost local search rankings
- Detailed feedback about reliability and professionalism would justify his premium pricing
- Regular reviews could keep his business visible in local search results year-round

Tom's recent radiator replacement job perfectly illustrated this. The customer found James' business through Google, chose them based on reviews specifically mentioning radiator work, and booked immediately because recent reviews showed they were reliable. By doing one thing right, asking for a review, he had achieved three things at once: advertising his business, building trust with new customers, and turning inquiries into sales.

But the real power came from how these effects compounded:

- Higher search rankings brought more 'ready to buy now' opportunities
- Positive reviews about boiler servicing led to annual maintenance contracts
- Maintenance customers became boiler replacement customers years later
- Satisfied customers recommended James's company to neighbours
- Each new review strengthened this cycle further, building natural momentum

This same compounding effect works across all service businesses, from physiotherapy practices converting one-off treatments into care plans to B&Bs turning weekend stays into annual traditions. It isn't complicated SEO marketing or secret website tricks, just a more systemised collection of actual customer experiences.

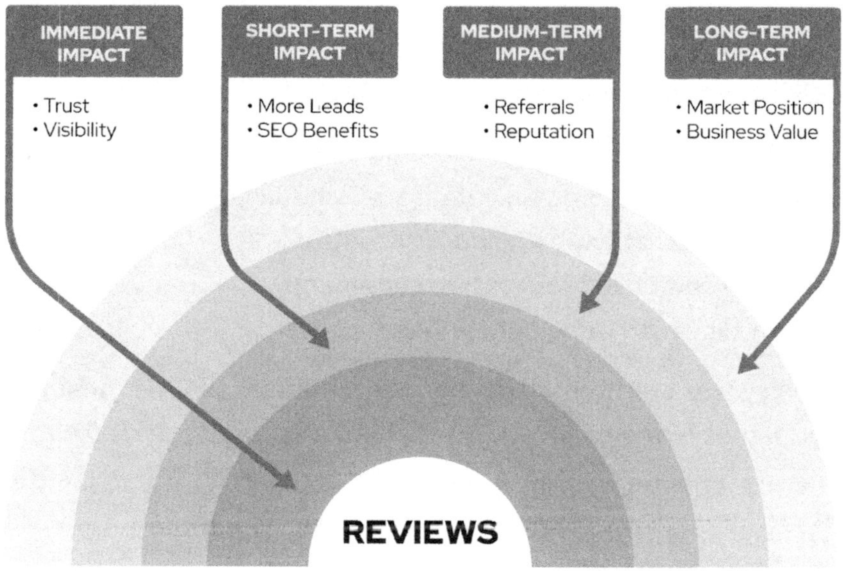

Fig 2.2: ***The Impact of Reviews on Your Business***

A properly implemented review system has rippling benefits the longer you systematically gather reviews. There are immediate trust and visibility gains (innermost ring). Then come lead generation and SEO benefits. As a body of reviews builds, it helps build a more substantial reputation and word-of-mouth referrals. Ultimately, reviews create a long-term market position and increase the value of the business to a prospective acquirer.

Break free from chaotic marketing and sales admin

"I could handle triple the work if I could just get out of my own way," James had told his accountant recently. He wasn't wrong. His feast-famine cycle was subtle but costly. Emergency calls kept him busy, but not always with client jobs. Admin and quotes stole hours that he could spend growing the business. Every day on the tools meant he postponed growth plans, and every unplanned call-out stopped him from improving his business.

James opened his project planner and began mapping what needed systemising first:

Critical Processes:

- Quote creation and follow-up
- Customer communication and scheduling
- Service delivery and quality control
- Review collection and management
- Local marketing and visibility

The key was starting with the process that caused the most pain. For James, streamlining quotes would free up evenings for more time with his family and days he could set aside for working on the strategic side, planning ways to grow his business. He pulled up a blank document and started simply:

- Create standard pricing template for typical jobs
- Build a simple process anyone could follow
- Test with the next month's quotes
- Track time savings and consistency
- Refine based on results

Within weeks of implementing this one system, his quote preparation time would halve. More importantly, he could see how the same systematic approach would transform other parts of his business. The potential was clear. One small system, properly implemented, would lead to more significant changes across his business.

Questions to consider

Take a few minutes to reflect on your current reality. These questions will help identify where thinking in systems could transform random activity into predictable success:

Scan the QR code to chat with HeyPip AI to get clarity and a tailored plan on this topic in your business.

lemonadeplan.com/ch2

1. What are your top three business processes that still depend entirely on you as the bottleneck? Rank them in order of how much time they consume.

2. What's stopped you in the past from creating a system for the activity you ranked as most time-consuming? Be specific about the barriers you have.

3. How much time outside your preferred working hours do you lose in a typical week to work that might be systemised?

Remember: Just as a heating system needs regular maintenance to run efficiently, business systems require attention to maintain effectiveness. The difference is that well-maintained business systems don't just prevent breakdowns, they create sustainable growth.

James began systemising his heating business one process at a time. Across town, another networking group member was facing his own challenges. Michael, the physiotherapist, was about to discover that his patient journey systems needed just as much attention as his treatment plans.

Part 2: The Current Reality

Chapter 3: The Customer Journey

"The customer's journey is at the heart of everything we do."

– Mary Barra, CEO of General Motors, history maker as the first female CEO of a major car brand

Scene: with Michael, the physio, at his private practice

Michael's last physiotherapy patient of the day, Rachel, had just left. He'd just completed her discharge following her final session. In just a few months, Michael had guided her from chronic back pain to being able to take part in pilates classes again. Moments like this were why he'd spent all those years training to become a physio.

Rachel spent three months reading his blog posts, watching exercise videos, and saying, "I'll just give it another week," before a friend's recommendation finally convinced her to try it.

A notification from his CRM (Customer Relationship Management software) caught his attention: two new email enquiries about treatment. New enquiries used to give him a buzz of excitement. But more recently, as his business costs went up and patients became more careful with their money, the excitement had been replaced by a dread of 'not screwing up' new enquiries.

The numbers for last quarter told a stark story: fifty-seven enquiries, but only nine became patients. "How many Rachels am I missing?" Something wasn't working between that first tentative enquiry and booking a treatment.

Michael's phone buzzed with a message from Sarah – his business coach friend and recent patient: "Thanks for helping with my neck last week. Those exercises are really working."

"Glad to hear it. Keep up with it," Michael replied. "Hey, can I ask you a quick work question?"

"Sure, go for it!"

"What was my marketing like before you became a patient?"

Silence. No response. Michael wondered if Sarah was too embarrassed to tell him his marketing was terrible. Then came the reply: "You clearly explained my treatment plan when we met. But I'm not sure I'd have become a patient if I hadn't known you. I wouldn't have booked if we hadn't spoken because I didn't understand what you could do for me."

"Oh, what do you mean?"

"Well, you've got all these patient success stories like mine and patient care plans like you took me through face to face. But your website jumps straight to 'Book Now'. I'd have felt a bit put off."

Sarah was right. Just as treatments like her neck mobility exercises were gradual, his marketing needed to help people understand their condition first.

"Think about it." Sarah messaged. "You looked after me well as a patient. Maybe use those same skills in your marketing?"

Meet Your Buyers Where They Are

Michael stared at his treatment notes from the week. Every patient journey followed a careful progression, from initial pain management to fully functional movement. No skilled physiotherapist would rush a patient straight to advanced exercises.

Yet his marketing did just that, jumping straight to 'Book Now', nothing else.

Rachel's initial email from five months ago showed the stark evidence:

"Hi, I've been experiencing increasing back pain for the last few months, especially in the morning. I'm unsure what's causing it. Could it be my mattress or my job?"

His response? "Thanks for your enquiry. I charge £75 for a 45-minute initial consultation. You can book online here..."

"No wonder she waited three months before booking. I'm surprised she did at all!" Michael grumbled. She'd been trying to understand her problem, and he'd jumped straight to selling a treatment. Just as he'd map out a patient's recovery journey, from pain management through to prevention, he needed to map the journey from first awareness to becoming a patient:

Pain and Confusion

→ Understanding

→ Research

→ Comparison

→ Decision

→ Treatment

Why hadn't he seen it this way before? It was like a physical rehab process. He would never leave a patient without support or education. And that's what he needed to provide in his marketing: systems that helped prospective patients understand their problems and progress towards booking care.

The Hidden 98%

Michael pulled up his website analytics, focusing on his most-viewed content. Only 20 people had read his featured article 'Unlock Peak Performance: Advanced Core Stability Exercises For Athletes' this year.

The pattern was painfully clear. He focused his content almost entirely on treatment and booking – perfect for the 2% ready to start physiotherapy. Meanwhile, the other 98% asked more fundamental questions when they left comments:

- "Could my desk job be causing this?"
- "When do I need professional help?"
- "Why aren't basic stretches working?"

Last month's posts told the story of misaligned priorities:

- "Advanced Exercise Tips" → 3% engagement
- "Book Your Consultation Today" → 1% click-through
- "Holiday Offer on Treatment" → 2% response

He remembered that his web designer added a tool that showed how people used his website. "Heat mapping," he'd called it. It shows where website visitors click and spend time on pages. Michael dug out the login details buried deep in his inbox archive. The website data showed what was going wrong: people were scrolling past his booking calls-to-action, searching for answers to basic questions. One of the most-viewed pages after the homepage? The one blog post about morning back pain he'd written months ago: ten times the engagement, with readers spending an average of six minutes understanding their condition. But there is no 'Download This Guide' form on the page, just another 'Book Now' button.

"I'm not only getting content wrong for people who enquire," he realised. "I'm probably turning away hundreds of potential patients who aren't ready to make a treatment enquiry yet."

Build systematic paths

"I need to treat my content like a treatment plan," Michael said as he opened his notes app. The same principles that guided patient rehabilitation could transform his content strategy.

Like Rachel's transformation, his most successful patients always got better by following a clear progression. Now, his content needed to do the same:

Early Understanding (like initial pain assessment):

- Simple explanations about what causes back pain
- Simple self-tests
- "Is this normal?" guidance → Helping people understand and trust you

Finding Solutions (like treatment planning):

- Treatment comparisons
- Professional help indicators
- Recovery timeframes
- Signs of improvement → Creating informed decisions

Ready to Start (like starting treatment):

- Patient success stories
- Step-by-step explanations of treatments
- Team expertise → Natural progression to booking

Systematic nurture design

Michael opened his email software, frowning at his current follow-up sequence: a welcome message, basic guide delivery, then silence.

"I'm doing exactly what I tell patients not to do," he sighed as he clicked into one of his recent client's aftercare programmes. Every patient's recovery followed a natural pattern. Early sessions focused on pain management, and later ones on building strength and confidence. Why did his email sequence not follow the same progression? "Why do I warm them up and leave them to go cold?"

When Michael looked at his most successful treatment cases, such as Rachel's, he realised that his email education series could mimic a similar progression to that series of patient sessions. The early days needed quicker, confidence-building wins, then gradually increasing gaps as understanding grew and questions evolved:

Day 1-4: Building trust (like initial pain management)

- Welcome and guide delivery
- Quick tips they could implement
- Early confidence builders

Days 7-20: Growing understanding (like building basic movement patterns)

- Deeper education about causes
- Explaining how treatments work
- Success markers

Days 33-89: Natural progression (like advancing to functional movement)

- Case studies showing the transformation
- Treatment comparison guidance
- Decision support

Make it systematic

Michael pulled up his patient progress tracker, which he religiously checked for patient progress. "If I track every minor improvement in patient mobility," he thought, "why aren't I tracking my communication effectiveness?"

He created a simple tracking system, familiar territory for someone used to monitoring recovery milestones:

Response Markers (like early treatment indicators):

- How many people read each email
- Download completion rates

Progress Signals (like movement assessments):

- Visiting key pages
- Reading patient stories
- Email clicks or replies

As he looked at tomorrow's schedule, Michael felt a new purpose. His first appointment was with a patient who downloaded his back pain guide two weeks ago. Thankfully, this patient trusted him enough to book independently, so his process wasn't entirely broken. But he wondered how many more enquiries he could turn into patients if he had more carefully crafted follow-up messages.

"Treatment plans need regular adjustment based on patient response," he typed into his notes. "This education sequence will need the same care and attention."

He blocked out two hours of focused time each morning for the next week. The first step was reorganising his 'morning back pain' content into the email sequence he'd mapped out. Just like rehabilitation, small, consistent actions would build towards a more significant transformation.

When Michael opened a new guide request that had just arrived, he smiled. Instead of his usual rushed "here's how to book" response, he could trust his sequence to build understanding systematically, just like a properly structured treatment plan.

Questions to consider

Take a moment to reflect on your business. Don't worry if you don't know the specifics, but try to imagine yourself in the shoes of your client, patient, or guest.

Scan the QR code to chat with HeyPip AI to get clarity and a tailored plan on this topic in your business. lemonadeplan.com/ch3

These questions will help you identify where your current marketing strategy might be missing opportunities to build a systematic understanding of potential clients.

1. Think about your customers from the moment they first realise they have a problem until they decide to buy from you.

- ➢ What kind of information do they look for?
- ➢ What questions do they ask their friends?
- ➢ What help do they need?
- ➢ How could your website and social media help?

2. Imagine you're someone who just discovered they have the kind of problem your business solves.

- What would you want to know first?
- What would help you understand the problem better?
- What could you share in blogs, videos, or guides that would help people who are not ready to buy yet?

3. Think about people you know who could use your help but haven't contacted you yet.

- What could you put on your website to get their email address?
- What helpful information could you send them to show how you could help?

Just as lemonade loses its fizz, unloved leads lose interest and momentum in the journey to becoming a customer. Your education sequence of emails should build trust systematically, guiding people naturally through understanding their problems and how they might consider ways to address them rather than pushing for immediate commitment.

We've seen the importance of matching content to customer readiness with Michael. In Chapter 4, The Strategy Gap, we'll see how Emma, a virtual assistant, faces her systems challenge. Emma discovers that knowledge without putting ideas into action creates bottlenecks. Her story reveals how expertise can become a barrier to progress.

Chapter 4: The Strategy Gap

"Strategy without tactics is the slowest route to victory. Tactics without strategy is the noise before defeat."

- Sun Tzu, ancient Chinese military strategist, philosopher, and the author of 'The Art of War'

Scene: with Emma, the virtual assistant, in her office

Emma minimised another browser tab, another webinar about the latest project management app, which she added to her growing and laughably long collection of 'must-implement' tools. Her browser history told the story: 'New AI Automation Apps', 'Latest CRM Comparison', 'Top 10 Productivity Tools', and 'Ultimate Client Portal Setup'. Her Notes app overflowed with feature lists and integration possibilities copied from countless webinars and product demos.

She glanced at her calendar, where client work filled the spaces predictably enough. But she'd fallen into the trap of trying to master every new tool and technique her clients might need. Instead of focusing on what worked, she had fourteen different versions of her tech stack document, each more 'perfect' than the last, and still hadn't implemented any of them in her business.

Her mouse hovered over another 'Game-Changing Automation Platform' demo. This one could have the missing piece her clients needed. She caught herself and laughed darkly. The missing piece, she realised, wasn't about watching another demo. It was doing anything with the mountain of tools she already knew worked.

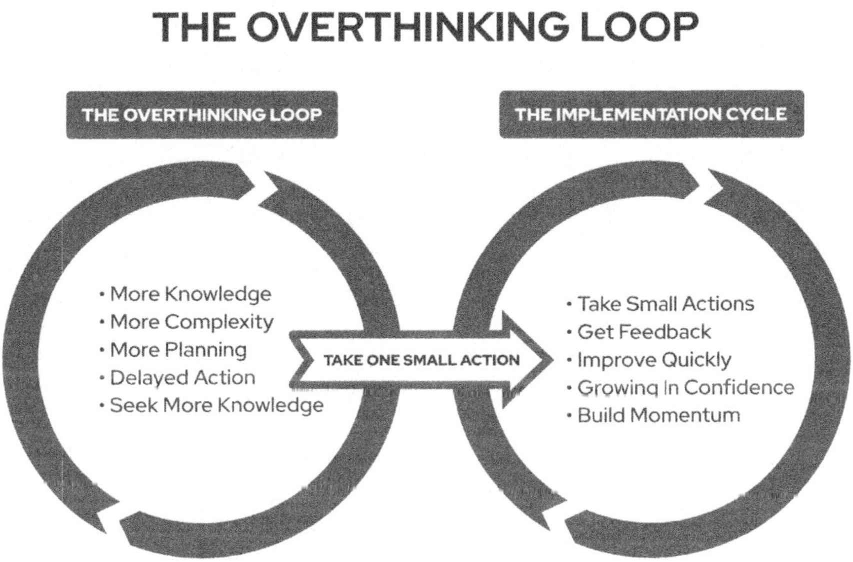

Fig 4.1: ***The Overthinking Loop***

The left loop (**The Overthinking Loop**) shows a common situation that experts in their fields get stuck in. When you get stuck in overthinking and inaction, continuing to accumulate knowledge can lead to complexity, over-planning and more delayed action.

A breakpoint between the circles shows how taking one small action can transform overthinking into implementation success: When you're in **The Implementation Cycle**, taking small purposeful actions leads to real-time feedback, which builds confidence and creates business momentum.

The Overthinking Loop

Perhaps you recognise yourself in Emma's story. The endless consumption of 'how-to' content. The growing collection of strategies that never quite make it from plan to reality. The constant feeling that you just need to learn one more thing before you're ready to implement.

Welcome to **The Overthinking Loop** - where your knowledge blocks your progress rather than being an enabler of it.

Here's the painful truth about expertise: The more you know, the more you realise how much could go wrong. Every time you learn something new, you add another layer of complexity to consider. Another factor to optimise. Another variable to perfect before launching.

The result? Analysis paralysis wrapped in the comfort blanket of "professional development."

Consider the typical pattern:

- **Monday**: Watch YouTube videos on Facebook ads
- **Tuesday**: Decide Facebook ads aren't the answer, research LinkedIn
- **Wednesday**: Discover email marketing might be better
- **Thursday**: Wonder if messaging needs work first
- **Friday**: Question your niche and positioning
- **Saturday**: Start planning a podcast (it worked for someone else!)
- **Sunday**: Back to YouTube for podcast tutorials

This vicious circle particularly traps intelligent owners. It's one of the curses of expertise. Quick fixes do not solve underlying problems. Trained experts spend too much time thinking about every possible problem instead of taking action. Over-planning creates barriers to implementation. And so the cycle begins again.

Endless planning looks like smart business, but it isn't. But shouldn't you research thoroughly before acting? Shouldn't you learn from others' mistakes? Shouldn't you plan carefully?

Yes, but.

If you consider your zone of expertise the bullseye on a dartboard, many experts know more than their clients on topics outside that core zone. It's tempting to say 'yes' to helping clients with these topics 'because you probably could'.

This is a fool's errand. Whenever you say 'yes' to work outside your core expertise, you're saying 'no' to working with clients at what you do best. You can't deliver it systematically, scale it, or train others to deliver it consistently. Most concerningly, you risk delivering less value than you could with your actual expertise.

It isn't just about capability. It's about systematic delivery. Stepping outside your core expertise makes you lose time, money, reputation, and, ultimately, client trust.

The Implementation Advantage

While you're planning your perfect podcast launch, someone else has already recorded ten imperfect episodes and learnt what their audience wants. Similarly, while perfecting your email sequence, another business owner sent their "good enough" version to 100 prospects and received real feedback.

Emma's phone beeped. It was James: "Hi Emma – thanks for the referral to Mrs Baxter. Much appreciated. Oh, and that booking tool you mentioned last time: I started using it yesterday."

"Already? I thought you were still researching options?"

"Trusted you and didn't have time to spare. Like when we get on site for a full system replacement, you have to start somewhere. Radiators in first, pipework, then boiler and controls. Nobody likes staying cold. Went with your booking tool and got on with it."

"And?"

"Decent. Maybe 80% perfect. 3 bookings already. Better than sending emails and texts back and forth like appointment booking tennis!"

Emma stared at her collection of automation research. While she'd been planning the perfect system, James had just started somewhere and launched what mattered.

The implementation advantage is simple: getting honest customer feedback is better than endless planning, market response trumps research, client reality overrules expert assumptions, and taking action builds momentum.

Break the overthinking loop

The path out of the expertise trap isn't through more knowledge – it's through systematically implementing what you already know. It doesn't mean abandoning strategy or expertise. Instead, it means using them in service of action rather than as a barrier to it.

Emma saw this most painfully in the "cliff-drop moment", when client enthusiasm peaks during the sales process and plummets right after they've paid. She'd invest enormous energy in discovery calls and proposal creation, building genuine excitement about the transformation ahead. Then, after the client signed, there was silence. The same perfectionism that led to her endlessly refining her sales process meant she hadn't yet developed a systematic onboarding process.

"I'll send a proper welcome pack once I've perfected it," she told herself as her new clients wondered if they'd made the right decision. Their excitement and momentum from the sales meetings vanished into the growing gap between her perfect plans and actual implementation.

She understood the cruel irony. Just yesterday, she'd helped a client with a simple lead magnet, a basic PDF guide with a follow-up email sequence. It had already attracted new clients. No studying email marketing for six months, perfecting design through endless revisions, or researching every possible automation tool. They'd created a helpful guide, set up a simple sequence, and started collecting leads immediately.

The difference? Emma had previously trained them to understand that momentum beats perfection every time. Do as I say, not as I do.

The virtuous circle of implementation

When you shift from endless planning to systematic implementation, something interesting happens. You create a virtuous circle:

- Small actions create immediate feedback.
- You use that feedback to make things better.
- Seeing improvements makes you more confident.
- Confidence enables more significant actions.
- And success creates momentum.

It works because you act based on what has happened, not what you think might happen. Every small step moves you closer to what will work for your business.

Build implementation habits

You need to build new habits to shift from endless planning to consistent implementation:

- Take one small step toward your goal every day
- Do not plan the next day's action until you have completed today's task
- Collect real feedback
- Improve things based on how they work in real life
- Document progress

Weekly: Review what worked and what didn't. Gather feedback. Plan your next small step. Keep momentum building.

Moving forward

As we explore the components of the LEMONADE Plan in the next chapter, remember that the framework itself isn't the answer. Implementing it is. Implementing even part of your plan works better than having a perfect plan you never use.

Emma finally closed her YouTube tab and opened her email platform. "Good enough and done," she thought, setting up a basic welcome sequence for new subscribers. It wasn't perfect. It wasn't even close to what she ultimately envisioned. But it was about to be something her perfect strategy had never been:

Actually running.

Questions to consider

Take a few moments to reflect on your planning-to-action ratio. Be honest with yourself – the sooner you recognise that you are stuck in the expertise trap, the easier it becomes to break free:

Scan the QR code to chat with HeyPip AI to get clarity and a tailored plan on this topic in your business. lemonadeplan.com/ch4

1. Where are you using "I need to learn more" as an excuse to delay action?

2. What's the simplest version of your big plan you could launch now, not next week, not after more planning, but today?

Take action now

Before moving on, commit to one small implementation step. It might be to:

- Send that email you've drafted six times
- Set up a basic booking link
- Create a simple lead magnet
- Ask your next client for a review
- Start a basic follow-up sequence

Remember: Just as lemonade loses its fizz if left sitting too long, perfect plans go flat without implementation. It's time to add some sparkle through action.

Hi! Did you take one of those action steps from the last page before you moved on?

If nothing changes, nothing changes.

If you need further inspiration or help, get a priority sequence in place by chatting with HeyPip here:

lemonadeplan.com/ch4

Scan the QR code to chat with HeyPip AI to get clarity and a tailored plan on this topic in your business.

lemonadeplan.com/ch4

OK, let's continue...

Part 3: The Bridge

Chapter 5: A System for Success

"The system is the solution."

– Lisa Su, CEO renowned for transforming AMD computer processors into a leader in high-performance computing

Scene: with Sarah, the business coach, in her office

Sarah stood back from her whiteboard, studied the client journey map she'd drawn and took a sip of lemonade. The fizzy bubbles from twenty minutes ago were flat – much like many of the recent sales opportunities in her business.

Sarah knew the scope of the transformation ahead was significant. She'd learned that changing from 'best efforts' to 'effective systems' isn't easy, and she had seen this by helping other businesses do the same thing (but with more resources at their disposal). However, continuing with random activities would be more challenging in the long run. Like any significant change, success comes from making the right moves in the right order.

Her diagram spanned the board, tracking a client's path from first contact to becoming a vocal advocate. After fifteen years of helping other businesses to grow, she'd mapped countless journeys. When businesses connected all the parts correctly, they succeeded. When they missed steps or did them poorly, opportunities went flat. "Just like that lemonade," she thought.

The gaps in her own business were painfully evident. Despite excellent discovery calls, she had no systematic way to nurture leads who weren't ready to book. They simply drifted away. Even worse, the momentum from sales conversations fizzled out after payment. New clients sat in limbo between signing and starting, their enthusiasm fading into uncertainty.

Her delivery lacked consistency. Some clients received detailed session notes and clear action steps, while others received hurried summaries between calls. The results spoke for themselves. She had just three Google reviews in the past year. Her best clients rarely gave her the testimonials she needed because the systems to create and capture them didn't exist.

Looking back at her whiteboard, Sarah understood that success wasn't about perfecting any individual element. It was about building joined-up systems that kept that "fizz" throughout the client journey.

She'd just encountered the importance of LEMONADE Planning...

LEMONADE Plan

Just as lemonade loses its fizz, so do your relationships with your leads and customers. LEMONADE Plan is a joined-up system that helps you manage eight critical business processes. It consistently generates leads, sales, upsells, and endorsements in a way that easily scales as you grow.

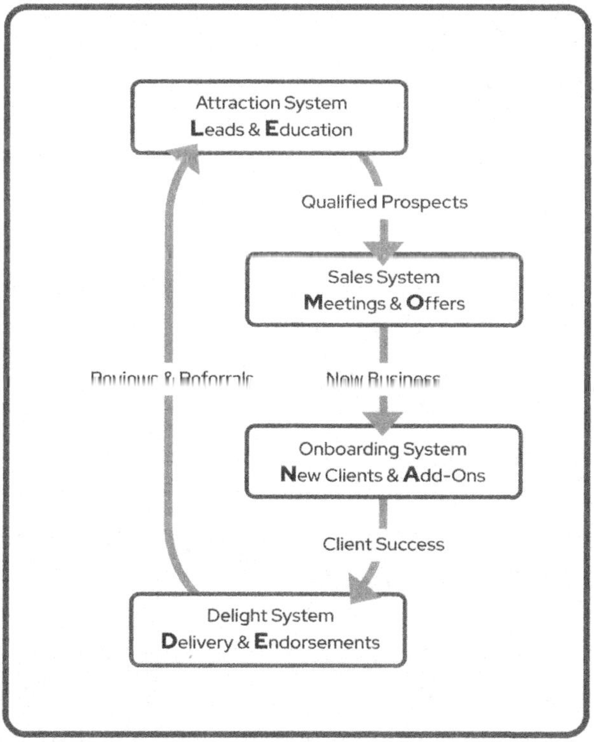

Fig 5.1: ***LEMONADE Plan: Four Systems, Eight Processes***

Each system works together in a continuous loop and helps the next one work better, creating a growth cycle. **Attraction** brings in qualified prospects, **Sales** converts them effectively, **Onboarding** expands their value, and **Delight** generates the reviews and referrals that power more **Attraction**.

Let's explore each process in more detail:

L: Lead Generation – Turn more interest into leads

Without predictable and consistent lead targeting, generation, and capture processes, you can't be sure you'll turn enough people who visit your website into people interested in buying from you. How happy are you with your methods for finding new clients? Do your online and offline methods work well together?

E: Education – Patiently nurture until you're the obvious choice

98% of visitors to your website aren't ready to buy yet. If you only focus on the other 2% who are ready for a quote, a meeting or a treatment now, you're missing out on almost all the buyers who might be ready in the next few weeks, months, or even years.

M: Meetings – Book meetings and prep your prospect for success

You only have so many hours in your day, so it's essential that the time you invest in meeting with potential clients is effective and leads to predictable results. How and when prospects book time in your diary and how you prepare them for it in the run-up should make both of you feel confident that you're in the right place.

O: Offers – Make compelling offers quickly and profitably

Almost every successful small business has a signature product, product line, or service that accounts for most of its revenues and profits. Your marketing, sales conversations, and quote templates should address the customer problems that your signature offer solves. You'll also have electronic payment services ready to accept payments into your bank account.

N: New Clients – Set realistic expectations as you welcome new clients

How you welcome new customers into your business can affect your chances of landing glowing reviews, case studies, or referrals. After taking payment, if the customer senses that you haven't carried your sales momentum and energy into the delivery phase, any fizz quickly disappears. It's a cliff-drop moment.

A: Add-Ons – Turn first-time clients into repeat ones

When you have sales conversations, you should listen or look for clues about how you can help them more after solving their first problem. If you know you could help them more, it's your duty to do so. It means being able to sell to them again, even better if it fits an existing upsell or add-on package you offer.

D: Delivery – Provide the service for what you've sold

In your small business, reputation is everything. It's critical to deliver what you say you will, when you promised it, and how you promised to do it. If you're unclear about what you'll deliver, customers will expect different things and be disappointed.

E: Endorsements – Turn client delight into reviews and warm referrals

Your work in the previous seven steps determines how likely you are to get positive reviews, referrals or case studies. Do them poorly or inconsistently, and you've no chance. The worst gaps appear when the sales experience delivers more than the new client experience. But if you maintain high quality from lead to completion and everything in between, your clients will honour the help you've given them by giving five-star reviews and warm referrals to others like them.

Just as lemonade loses its fizz if left unattended, so do your relationships with your leads and customers. LEMONADE Plan is the joined-up system that helps you manage eight critical processes in your business; processes that consistently generate leads, sales, upsells, and endorsements in a way that scales as you grow.

Implement in Reverse

Sarah stared at her diagram, something nagging at her thoughts. The client journey made perfect sense, left to right, from Leads to Endorsements, because that is what it is: 'the client's journey.' However, small businesses often fail when they try to build these systems in this order without having separate teams able to work on preparing multiple processes to be ready at the same time.

'What am I trying to achieve here?' she murmured, reaching for a fresh marker. She thought back to that 'Perfect Review' document she'd created previously – the glowing testimonials she wanted. Maybe she needed to work backwards from there. She began drawing on the whiteboard again, this time starting from the right-hand side.

To get those reviews, she needed to consistently deliver exceptional results. To deliver consistently, she needed the right offers she could systematically fulfil. First, she needed to perfect her delivery and offers. Then, she could find the perfect add-on services to create natural growth opportunities.

Only after all of that was clear, did it make sense to focus on lead generation. Then Sarah would know who she was looking for and what she could systematically deliver to them. Their education would focus on the journey to her proven solutions. Sales meetings would become more productive because she would know the specific offer she was selling and to whom. The new client onboarding would align perfectly with her delivery systems.

"**EDOALEMN**," Sarah wrote at the bottom of her board. "Not as catchy as **LEMONADE**, but a much better way to build out these systems."

She outlined the implementation order:

1. **E**ndorsements: Start with the end in mind. What do you want your reviews to say? Who do you want referrals from?
2. **D**elivery: Consistently create endorsement-worthy experiences.
3. **O**ffers: Create packages that your delivery system can consistently fulfil.
4. **A**dd-Ons: Build natural expansions that enhance your core offer.
5. **L**eads: Now you know who you're looking for and what you can systematically deliver to them.
6. **E**ducation: Your content can focus on the journey to your proven solutions.
7. **M**eetings: Conversations become more productive because you know what offer you're selling and to whom.
8. **N**ew Clients: Onboarding aligns perfectly with your delivery systems.

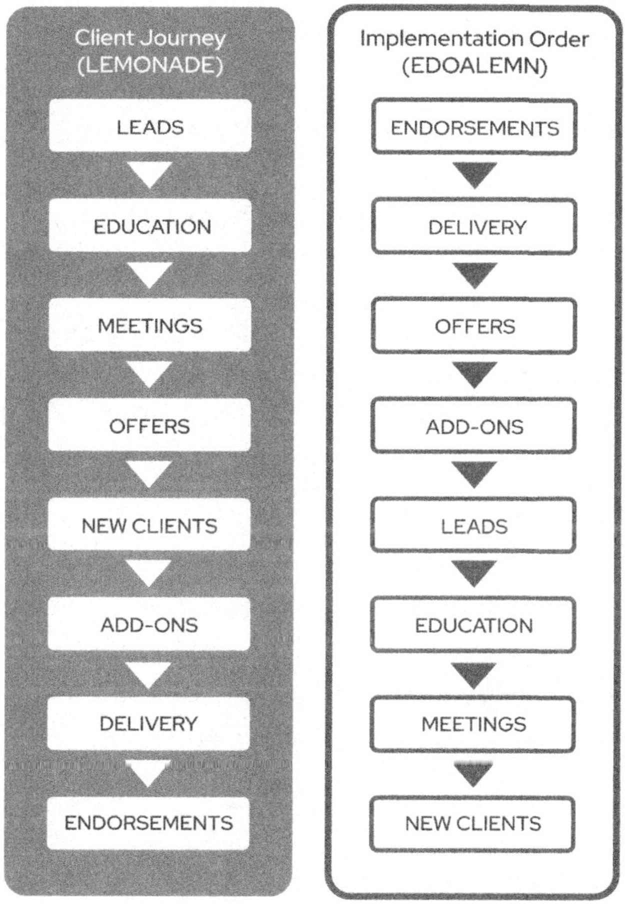

Fig 5.2: ***The Working Backwards Implementation Model***

Clients experience your business in the flow on the left-hand side (LEMONADE). But when you build these systems into your business it works better when you start with the end in mind (EDOALEMN). Starting with **Endorsements** helps define what you'll **Deliver**, which shapes your **Offers**, and so on. The working backwards implementation model makes sure that each new process supports the ones that follow in the client journey.

Why integration matters

Sarah sat back and looked at her whiteboard again. The **LEMONADE** parts and the **EDOALEMN** implementation order made sense, but she realised something even more fundamental: none of these systems could work properly in isolation.

A perfect delivery system couldn't generate endorsements if the onboarding process set unrealistic expectations. The best educational content would be wasted if it attracted leads who weren't ready to grow their practice. Even flawless lead generation would fall flat if the follow-up processes weren't aligned with Sarah's capacity.

> Two things matter here: making sure all your systems work together and keeping your clients excited throughout their journey. Like carbonation in a drink, pressure needs to be consistent. One underwhelming experience, misaligned connection, or gap in the process, and the fizz would escape.

Sarah created eight folders on her laptop – one for each process in LEMONADE – and began mapping how each system would feed into the next:

- Systematic delivery would make endorsements natural
- Clear offers would make delivery consistent
- Well-structured add-ons would grow client value
- Targeted leads would match her proven offers
- Educational content would nurture the right prospects
- Meetings would convert qualified opportunities
- New client onboarding would maintain momentum

Every link between systems was important. A gap between any two systems meant opportunities could slip through, fizz could be lost, and potential endorsements might never materialise.

When Sarah reviewed her current process, she could see where the fizz escaped. Her sales calls were excellent, but the fizz of that initial enthusiasm went flat without a proper way to welcome new clients. Her delivery could be outstanding, but those potential endorsements evaporated without a clear system for gathering reviews.

She began mapping the critical connection points:

- When a lead downloads a guide, what happens next?
- After they book a call, how do I prepare them for it?
- Once they pay, what's their first experience?
- During delivery, how is progress tracked?
- After key milestones, when are reviews requested?

Each step needed its own mini-process to keep clients excited. Like the bubbles in a drink, the whole client journey needs to keep its fizz. One disappointing link could ruin the entire experience.

Questions to consider

Before moving to Part 4, where we'll explore how to start implementation with systematic endorsements, take a moment to reflect:

Scan the QR code to chat with HeyPip AI to get clarity and a tailored plan on this topic in your business. lemonadeplan.com/ch5

1. If you mapped out your customer journey from the first touch to their review or referral, where would you find gaps where momentum gets lost and the 'fizz' escapes?

2. Thinking about your marketing:

- Does it align closely with your offer, what you deliver, and the endorsements you want?
- Where could you speak more specifically about the problems your market faces?

3. Which of the four systems needs the most attention in your business?

- ➢ Attraction (**L**eads & **E**ducation)
- ➢ Sales (**M**eetings & **O**ffers)
- ➢ Onboarding (**N**ew Clients & **A**dd-Ons)
- ➢ Delight (**D**elivery & **E**ndorsements)

4. Look at recent client experiences.

- ➢ At what points did enthusiasm peak and dip?
- ➢ What systems could you put in place to maintain momentum throughout their journey?

> Remember: Just as lemonade loses its fizz if left unattended, random business activities can't create sustainable success. It's time to add some systematic sparkle to your approach.

Now that we understand the complete LEMONADE framework, it's time to explore how to implement it – starting with the end in mind. In Part 4, we'll see how Michael's physiotherapy practice transformed when he began working backwards from systematic endorsements and how this approach can also work in your business.

Part 4: Work Backwards

Chapter 6: Systematic Endorsements

"Your most satisfied customer is your next best lead."

– Theo Paphitis, British retail entrepreneur and former Dragon's Den investor

Scene: with Michael, the physio, at his private practice

Michael stared at his website visitor numbers and felt proud but frustrated. His latest paid ads were getting clicks, and his exercise tips had decent social media engagement. But quietly outperforming both channels sat Jenny's review from last year – still bringing in new patients who searched for "morning back pain" and "physiotherapist near me."

Michael read another 'SEO Expert' article that promised "10 hacks to rank higher on Google," but his eyes glazed over at terms like "keyword density" and "meta descriptions." The irony struck him: while he'd been chasing technical solutions, Jenny's story of transformation from injured runner to marathon finisher had brought him more new patients than any marketing tactic.

"Hang on," he thought, suddenly understanding. Without any SEO expertise, Jenny had written precisely what potential patients searched for – no tricks, no technical optimisation, just her real experience in her own words.

That realisation made Rachel's missing review even more painful. Yesterday, he'd had his last appointment with her, marking the end of her remarkable transformation, from barely walking to confidently attending pilates classes. Her story would have been perfect for showing other chronic pain sufferers what was possible. But he'd never systematically asked for it, and now he'd lost that momentum.

Michael opened WhatsApp: "Hey Emma, quick question... How do you make sure you and your clients get reviews for your work?"

"Funny you ask. Used to be a disaster. Had a client last week remind me of the old days – their welcome emails went missing, and login details never arrived. Dead embarrassing when you're meant to be the organised one!"

"So what changed?"

"Mapped out where things should connect. Now, we track every milestone. When something's working well, we document it. Makes asking for reviews dead simple – the story's already there."

"Hmm. Like my patient notes and progress markers..."

"Exactly! You've already got it all. Just need that final step – turn those progress points into natural moments to capture the story. Same system, one extra step."

Michael glanced at Rachel's discharge notes. Emma was right. Everything he needed for a perfect review was sitting right there in his records.

Michael opened his practice management software and winced. Last month alone, he'd discharged ten patients successfully. Ten powerful transformations. Ten potential reviews that would help people find his practice on Google – and, more importantly, inform future patients – exactly how his practice changed lives. How many other Jennys and Rachels had slipped away without sharing their success?

"I don't need to chase SEO tricks," he said under his breath, creating a fresh document titled 'Review Collection System.' "I just need to capture these stories systematically before they slip away. The rest happens naturally."

The Hidden Power of Customer Stories

Michael spotted patterns he'd missed before as he scrolled through his discharge notes. Last month's successes told compelling stories:

- Vicky is back to crushing tennis serves after shoulder rehabilitation
- Four chronic pain patients transformed from daily struggle to newfound freedom
- A carpenter and nurse both returned to work without restrictions
- Mrs Thompson, 72, is now strong enough to chase her grandchildren

Each note showed how he changed people's lives, not just their health. Yet they sat hidden in Michael's files where they couldn't help new patients with similar problems.

Jenny's single review had quietly been bringing a drip of leads into his practice for months, bringing in runners with similar injuries. "One review did all that," he smiled, quickly working out the numbers. "What if I had ten? Twenty? A hundred stories systematically showing how we help people?" The potential wasn't just about marketing – it was about helping more people find the right help sooner.

Create stories worth sharing as reviews

Michael mapped out Rachel's journey in a new document called 'Systemised Review Collection,' focusing on when her enthusiasm peaked. These were the perfect moments to capture authentic testimonials naturally.

Michael saw a clear pattern:

1. Her first pain-free morning after three years of chronic discomfort
2. Returning to daily life: shopping, dog walks, full workdays without painkillers
3. Completing her first pilates class, proudly showing photos at her next session
4. The final assessment: comparing her remarkable progress to where she started

"These aren't just clinical milestones," he typed. "They're natural celebration points - perfect moments to capture authentic patient stories. But I need a proper system to track and act on these opportunities."

He sketched out a framework:

Celebration Points:

- Key progress markers
- Treatment milestones
- Goal achievements
- Transformation moments

Collection System:

- Progress tracking templates
- Celebration triggers

- Timing when to ask for the review
- Follow-up sequences – email, text
- Success story frameworks – what a success path looks like

The system wasn't pressuring patients for reviews but systematically recording how happy they were when they reached meaningful goals. Michael documented how every patient journey should build toward natural endorsements:

Before Treatment:

- First website impression: visitor sees success stories
- Educational content: weaving in real-life transformations
- Initial enquiry: setting care expectations
- Pre-appointment: building confidence through examples

During Treatment:

- First consultation: documenting starting points clearly
- Treatment planning: setting measurable markers
- Progress tracking: celebrating consistent wins
- Regular reassessment: measuring transformation
- Discharge preparation: building final comparison

After Treatment:

- Maintenance support: sustaining success
- Progress check-ins: maintaining the connection
- Success sharing: making reviews natural
- Community building: connecting stories

"Every touchpoint needs a system," Michael realised. He could improve each step with moments worth sharing from previous patients' feedback. The more he showed that happy patients built his practice's reputation, the more naturally prospective patients could imagine their role in continuing this tradition.

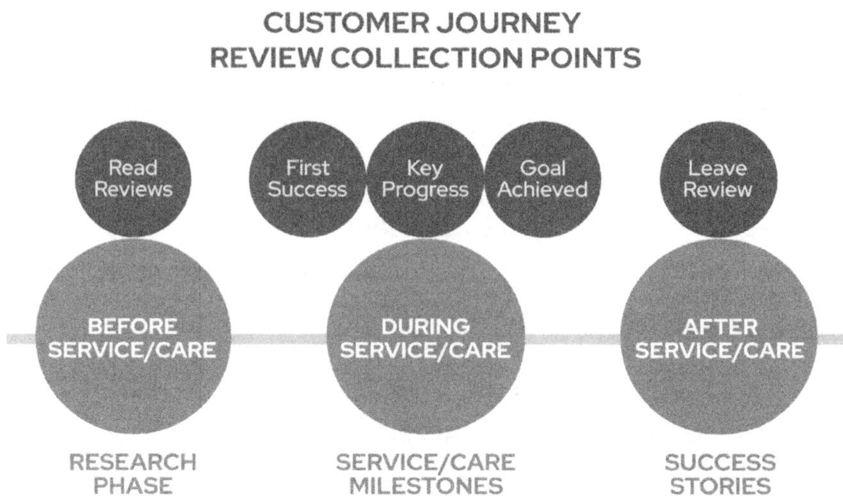

Fig 6.1: ***The Role of Reviews in the Customer Journey***

This shows key moments for review collection and use, from prospective clients or patients first reading others' reviews that mirrored their pain points to them sharing their success stories. Michael used this to identify natural points where patients were most likely to share their experiences, particularly after achieving significant progress or completing treatment goals.

The Natural Search Effect

Studying Jenny's review more closely, Michael spotted something fascinating. Without any guidance, she had naturally used exactly the phrases potential patients searched for: "lower back pain," "morning stiffness," and "running injuries." She had written in their language because she had been in their position.

Even more valuable, she mentioned both her specific problem and his location ("physio in [area]"), creating perfect local relevance. Each new review added another location reference, another condition description, and another treatment outcome, automatically updating his practice's visibility.

Better still, he realised that every new review would show Google that he helped his patients get better. Unlike his website, which rarely changed, reviews provided fresh, regular updates showing his practice helping more and more people. These authentic reviews quietly outperformed his website content in search results. For a few months, they even pushed his practice into Google's coveted "3-pack", those three local businesses shown more prominently at the top of maps and search results pages, showing reviews and contact details.

"No SEO tricks needed," he noted. "Just real patients sharing real transformations in their own words."

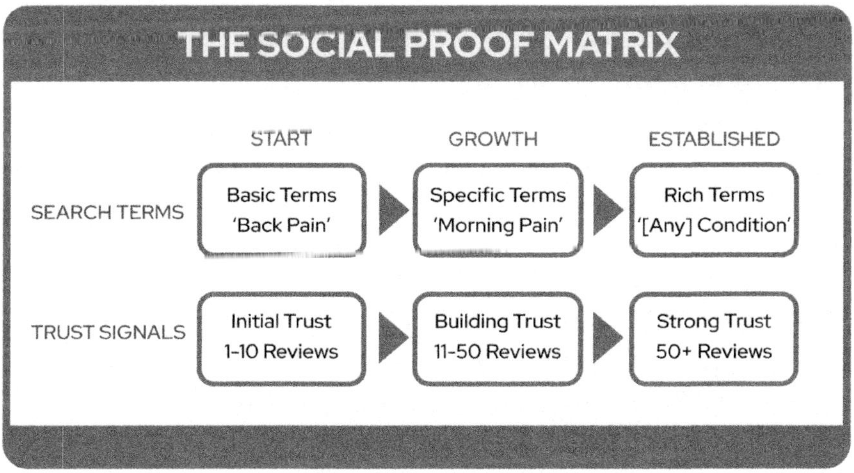

Fig 6.2: ***The Social Proof Matrix***

Multiple reviews organically build search visibility and trust over time. Michael saw how Jenny's single review contained valuable search terms for 'back pain', but a collection of reviews would cover more important keywords and build stronger credibility online.

Build momentum through success stories

Michael created two columns in a spreadsheet: 'key metrics' and 'impact measures'. He needed to measure the impact of the new review process.

Key Metrics:

- Number of weekly review requests sent out
- New reviews published
- Percentage of responses vs requests
- Types of care mentioned in reviews, e.g. lower back pain

Impact Measures:

- Website traffic
- New patient enquiries
- Conversion rates from enquiries to bookings
- Local search position, with a target to get on the "Google Maps 3-Pack"

Creating the spreadsheet felt good. It would help Michael measure the impact of his patient care efforts and remind him to ask for reviews at the right time. He named the spreadsheet 'Reviews Tracker' and saved it to Google Drive.

Make it happen

Michael spotted three discharge appointments in his diary for tomorrow, perfect timing for implementing his ideas. He sketched a simple but repeatable process for capturing each patient's success story.

Before the appointment, he would review the treatment plan and create a summary so the patient would understand how far they'd come. He would also provide an ongoing maintenance plan of exercises and reminders to help the patient continue their recovery, showing that he cared about their complete recovery.

During the appointment, it was essential to reflect on the little victories the patient had achieved, their work, and the patience they'd shown to achieve them. Doing this would help Michael introduce ways to prevent injury and setbacks in the future.

Face-to-face, he'd ask them to share how happy they were with the service by leaving a review to help others in a similar situation find Michael's service. After they left, he would send a personalised thank-you email with their review invitation. The email would include other helpful resources for maintaining progress. He would also schedule a follow-up check to maintain that systematic care connection.

The bigger picture

As Michael saved his notes, he realised that reviews would have multiple benefits. Reviews would attract new patients, build trust before the first visit, help uncertain sufferers decide to seek care and show newcomers what transformation looked like. Each story would add to a collection of success stories demonstrating that change was possible.

Michael felt energised as he looked at tomorrow's discharge appointments with fresh eyes. These weren't just endings anymore. They were opportunities to capture success stories that could guide others to get help sooner.

Michael looked again at his Google Business Profile and wondered how it would look in six months. Jenny's story wouldn't be sitting there alone. There would be dozens of other health transformations, each naturally pointing new patients to his practice. He wouldn't need to hire external marketing help or understand SEO's 'dark arts'; it would just be stories of real change, captured as part of a process and shared with the world.

Michael could see the connection. When he made collecting reviews part of a process, it was about more than marketing. It was also an opportunity for his clients to demonstrate how his physiotherapy practice delivered consistently high levels of care. Each testimonial would be an authentic and unique story of a patient's health transformation.

Now, he needed to ensure every treatment journey was worth celebrating. In Chapter 7, we'll see how James, the heating engineer, discovered that quality delivery creates reviews worth collecting.

The outcome pledge as a business mindset

If you don't collect success stories, it's harder for future clients to find you. Most businesses fall into one of three categories:

- they ask for and receive reviews consistently;
- they do so sporadically, perhaps because a process is missing, or they need more staff training, or;
- they hardly ever or never collect reviews

I've had clients who have spent significant sums of money with me who have been delighted with the work – and have regularly told me they are delighted with it – but who "just never got around" to leaving a review. Every time I had failed to follow my sales process properly, any combination of:

- I hadn't proactively introduced reviews into the discussion;
- I hadn't shown them reviews from happy clients or, even better, case studies;
- or I hadn't explicitly framed what I call the **'outcome pledge'** at a sales meeting.

The outcome pledge is simply a verbal request like:

"Hey, most of our new business comes from happy clients' referrals, reviews, or case studies. You probably saw some before we started working together. If we achieve what you are looking for here, would you also be open to sharing your experience through a quick review, a case study, or by introducing us to others who could benefit from what we do?"

Questions to consider

Before moving to Chapter 7, reflect on your review collection opportunities:

Scan the QR code to chat with HeyPip AI to get clarity and a tailored plan on this topic in your business.

lemonadeplan.com/ch6

1. What key moments in your client's journey deserve celebration with them?

2. Where are you missing opportunities to capture success stories?

➢ What system could you create to ensure no success story goes untold?

3. How could you make review requests feel more natural?

4. What would your perfect review say? Think about:

- Their concerns before working with you
- How you made them feel throughout
- The specific results they achieved
- Why they'd recommend you to others

Start building your review collection system this week with just one of these elements. Reviews work silently in the background, building trust and visibility whilst you focus on delivering excellent service. The key is having a system to capture them consistently.

Chapter 7: Quality Delivery

"If the old ways don't work, the new ways don't matter."

– Jason Fried, co-founder of Basecamp software and advocate of calm, remote-friendly work cultures

Scene: with James, the heating engineer, at his kitchen table

You on Your Best Day, Every Day

James re-read the Thompson's review for the third time:

> *"First-class from start to finish. James and his team were professional and thorough and left our home spotless. The pre-installation information was detailed and helpful. On the day, they documented everything with photos, explained what they were doing, and ensured we understood our new system completely. The follow-up call the next day was a lovely touch. Best of all, our house is finally warm throughout! If you need heating work, don't hesitate – this is how it should be done."*

That job had been everything he wanted his business to represent. Clear communication. Systematic installation. Thorough handover. Proper follow-up. He'd done everything right that day, but that was the problem – it had depended entirely on him.

James' kitchen table had a stack of job sheets scattered across it, and the contrast was stark. Tom's radiator installation for the Davies family earned just three stars, along with comments about inconsistent communication. They even mentioned how different their experience had been from their neighbour's installation just two months ago. Meanwhile, the Thompsons gave James' work five stars for essentially the same job.

James messaged Sarah, "Hey Sarah, how do you achieve the same level of satisfaction for each client when every client you help is different? What am I missing?"

"It definitely takes work," the response came, "but just had some feedback from a client saying how personal their leadership training felt. But my core training slides barely change from client to client."

"How's that work then?"

"Same as you really. Every house you work on is different, but they all need reliable heating. Every business I coach is different but needs the same leadership foundations. I've got a standard framework and training slides – I just pick examples that match each client's business."

James looked at Tom's job sheets, thinking about his successful system walkthrough with the Thompsons. If that approach worked so well, he needed to make it standard for every handover. Tom did excellent technical work, but he didn't document much. There were no photos of the finished installation, no clear notes about system settings, and no record of maintenance advice.

"I can't be on every job." He reached for his coffee. "But right now, every job delivery differs depending on who's there." His standards were clear in his head, but that was precisely the problem – he only kept them in his head.

Break down what excellence looks like

James opened a new document on his laptop and typed 'What Made The Thompson Job Perfect?' at the top. If he wanted every job to reach that standard, he needed to understand what had worked, and, more importantly, why.

He began breaking down the installation day. He had arrived early, giving himself time to review the site. Then came the crucial pre-start conversation, during which he confirmed the scope, checked access, and discussed the day's schedule. These weren't just formalities. They set the foundation for excellence.

Throughout the installation, he took photos at key stages to show the care taken. He updated Mrs. Thompson, maintaining that crucial connection even when working in different parts of the house. He immediately documented every variation from the quote to prevent any end-of-day surprises.

As James reviewed his regular work habits, he suddenly realised something important. He had not just developed random habits but carefully refined these processes to deliver quality results every time. He had just never written them down.

As he opened his CRM software, James began creating what he should have done months ago, a central set of standards that would eliminate the guesswork in every job. Instead of just using the system to schedule work, he could build these standards into it.

Build your communication framework

James looked at his CRM's settings menu. "Let's start with communication." The Thompson review had praised their pre-installation information, but achieving consistency meant creating proper templates rather than writing fresh emails for every job.

He clicked 'New Template' and began with the essentials, a pre-installation email the system would send when a client booked the job. It included clear instructions for parking and access requirements, installation day expectations, and team introductions. Photos of himself and Tom added the personal touch that made such a difference. A simple preparation checklist gave clients practical involvement in the process.

The app would prompt engineers through the key stages of their jobs. James created systemised professional communication steps – with relevant photos – triggered by confirmation of arrival, progress updates, and completion notices. Each update required just a few phone taps.

While testing the system, James sent himself a sample update. Moments later, it arrived clear and professional. The goal wasn't to create more work but to automate good communication, the same quality, delivered consistently.

Each message would start the next step automatically: pre-installation emails would launch internal checklists, completion notices would start follow-up sequences, and there would be a seamless flow from first contact to final sign-off.

"Standard doesn't have to mean impersonal," James realised, adding spaces for job-specific details. They could keep the same basic structure but change the details to match each client's job.

Trigger	Communication Step	Purpose	Key Elements
'Get quote' enquiry received	Initial response	Show that you're responsive	• Acknowledge receipt • Confirm next steps • Set response timeframe
After requirements gathered	Quote / proposal	Present solution	• Clear scope of work • Pricing / options • How to proceeed
Client books service	Booking confirmation	Set expectations	• Welcome message • What happens next • Any preparation needed
2-3 days before	Pre-service reminder	Final preparation	• Confirm time / location • Who they'll meet • What to bring / prepare
During service	Service delivery	Keep connected	• Progress updates • Next steps • Any decisions needed
Work complete	Service completion	Wrap-up	• What was completed • What happens next • Any maintenance / care needed
24-48 hrs afterwards	Follow-up	Build relationship	• Check satisfaction • Address any questions • Review / referral request
Per service schedule	Ongoing care	Maintain connection	• Maintenance reminders • Care tips / updates • Future booking prompts

Fig 7.2: ***The Delivery Communication Framework***

Each communication has a specific trigger point, purpose and content to ensure consistent client updates without relying on memory. When built into your CRM, these become automatic touchpoints that maintain momentum throughout service delivery. This example is from James' heating engineer business.

What would a similar grid look like in your business?

Document everything

James saw the issue when he opened a job folder from last week, one of Tom's installations. There were just three site photos and minimal notes. The technical work was excellent, but they could not prove it without proper documentation. More importantly, they had no record of system settings that clients might ask about later.

In contrast, James's folders contained fifteen to twenty photos documenting every stage, detailed setup notes, and specific maintenance guidance. The difference wasn't in technical skill. Tom was an excellent engineer. The gap was in knowing what to record and why.

Back at his desk, James opened the CRM and clicked on 'Create Workflow'. Here, he could build the documentation system through repeatable automation. For each new job, the CRM would create a sequence of required tasks, prompting for specific photos and information at key stages.

He mapped the core sequence: the pre-installation site condition, existing system documentation, installation progress shots, safety check evidence, final installation photos, and control panel settings. The system would keep each task open until the engineer added all the photos and notes, ensuring they didn't miss anything.

When James tested the system on a small radiator replacement, he discovered something unexpected: even he wasn't as consistent as he'd thought. He took some photos naturally but didn't include them in the tasks, and some of the other steps he'd listed weren't as crucial as he imagined.

By lunchtime, he had improved the checklist by arranging the steps in the order that made the most sense for the work. Completion tasks now included closeups of key safety checks and control settings, things he had done automatically but had not documented in the process.

Master the handover

The handover was where everything came together, or fell apart. James knew this from experience. Like the Davies job last month, it was a perfect installation, but Mrs Davies called three times that first week with questions about her controls. Each call revealed another gap: timer settings, room thermostats, and radiator valves, basic things the engineer should have explained on day one.

"We're making this too complicated," James realised. Handover wasn't about dumping technical knowledge on the client. It was about giving them confidence in their new system, showing them the essential controls, and ensuring they knew where to find help.

He set up a new task sequence in the CRM, breaking the handover into clear stages. He started with the basics, turning the heating on and off. He then moved to timer settings, walking through their daily routine. He helped them set comfortable temperatures. Finally, he explained the radiator valves and thermostat. Each step is built naturally on the one before it.

While working at the Thompsons, he learned something important. He had asked Mrs Thompson to try each heating control, watching as she adjusted settings and noting where she hesitated. Those moments of uncertainty were golden. They revealed what needed more explanation.

Most importantly, he added a final task: "Ask the client to explain in their own words how the settings work." This step helped build their confidence rather than testing them. When clients could tell him how their heating system worked using their own words, they rarely called for help later.

Tomorrow's job at the Hendersons would be perfect for testing. James had discussed it with Tom, who would handle it by following the new handover sequence in the CRM. Tom had a few questions but bought into the improvement ideas.

Systems that scale

The next afternoon, James watched from the kitchen doorway as Tom guided Mr. Henderson through the new controls. The difference was striking. Tom followed the checklist and confidently showed Mr Henderson each step, having him practice with the timer and temperature settings. When Mr Henderson hesitated over the frost protection settings, Tom spotted it immediately and offered a clearer explanation. Tom wasn't just following instructions. Tom delivered the same high-quality service that James would have given.

Afterwards, James caught up with Tom to congratulate him. He felt a surge of pride as he returned to his van. He'd just watched his business deliver outstanding service without him being directly involved. He reread the Thompson review on his phone: "...professional, thorough... detailed information... documented everything... made sure we understood our new system... follow-up call..." Back then, it had been a perfect job but also a one-off, James doing everything right on a good day. With proper systems in place, that level of service could become their standard.

This new understanding changed how he would package his offers. They could design each service package around how they'd systematically deliver it. The photo documentation, clear communication points, and thorough handover process weren't just procedures; they were selling points that set his service apart.

"We need to show this difference in our quotes," he thought. Installing a boiler wasn't just about the equipment anymore. It was about guaranteed quality checks, systematic testing, photographic evidence, and confident handover. He could justify premium pricing because he could prove precisely how their delivery method was better.

For standard installation services, maintenance contracts, and seasonal service plans, he could structure each offer around these systematic quality differences, knowing his team could consistently deliver, not just occasionally excel.

After all, you can only systematically sell what you can systematically deliver. And now, James could do both.

Delivery Process Elements	Business Impact	How it Links Back to Offers	How it Links Forward to Endorsements
The **quality standards** you set for yourself to deliver what you've sold	• Consistent service quality • Repeatable excellence • Clear team standards	High quality service shows you have absolute confidence in delivering what you include in your offer	Creates review-worthy experiences for your clients
Your **documentation**	• Evidence of care • Quality assurance / no tricks or shortcuts • Gives clients confidence in you	Mirrors back to what they've agreed to buy in your offer / proposal	Captures proof that what has been delivered is high quality
How you **communicate**	• Clear expectations • No surprises • Professional image	Supports premium pricing	Keeps client enthusiasm
How you **hand over** to the client, or complete the service	• Client satisfaction • Future business • Natural referrals	Creates opportunities to upsell	Creates moments for advocacy: referrals, reviews or case studies

*Fig 7.3: **Delivery Process Elements and Why You Need Them***

Every component of how you deliver what you have promised connects forward to earning endorsements and backwards to supporting your offers. The integration between the three processes (**O**ffers, **D**elivery, **E**ndorsements) ensures that what you promise in sales matches what you deliver in practice, creating a foundation for sustainable growth.

Questions to consider

Take a moment to reflect on your own business's delivery systems:

Scan the QR code to chat with HeyPip AI to get clarity and a tailored plan on this topic in your business.

lemonadeplan.com/ch7

1. Consider your perfect review from the last chapter and the standards your systems must consistently maintain. Are there specific quality markers it could praise about your client service delivery process?

2. Recall your best day – when everything worked perfectly. Were there valuable moments that 'just happened' you've never documented? These form the foundation of your delivery system.

3. Which parts of your service rely on team members "just knowing" what to do? What clear checklists would transform individual excellence into systematic quality?

4. What questions do clients ask when you're working with them or after the handover? How could a systematic process prevent these queries?

Remember: Quality isn't about doing extraordinary things – it's about doing ordinary things extraordinarily well every time. That only happens through systemisation.

In Chapter 8, we'll explore how to structure compelling offers that your delivery system can consistently fulfil. After all, as James discovered, you can only systematically sell what you can systematically deliver.

Chapter 8:
Make Compelling Offers

"Price is what you pay. Value is what you get."

– *Warren Buffett, investor, known for his straightforward wisdom on business and finance*

Scene: with Sarah, the business coach, in her office

The clutter on Sarah's desk showed that she was two teas, a coffee, a couple of crumbly HobNob biscuits[2] and a Dairy Milk chocolate bar into her current proposal – twelve pages of analysis, multiple packages, and customised solutions. She'd spent six hours crafting it for a prospect with five different challenges, attempting to solve them all.

Sarah glanced over at her "perfect review" she was hoping to land more of:

> *"Sarah transformed my accounting practice from a solo operation to a growing firm with three senior staff. Her structured approach helped me become a leader while maintaining quality. Within six months, I had clear growth plans, confident team management, and my first £30,000 month. I'm finally working ON my business, not*

2 For non-British readers, this is a popular British cookie, beloved for its crunchiness. A perfect snack for dipping (known as 'dunking') in a cup of tea, a very British tradition.

IN it. If you're an accountant ready to grow, work with Sarah."

Her diary showed three discovery calls tomorrow. Each would require hours of crafting custom proposals, which would consume her evenings while her conversion rate remained low.

"I'm treating every business like a puzzle." Sarah closed a tab of industry research. Her training had instilled a need to answer every question, but running a business was about creating predictable profits through systematic delivery.

She glanced at her whiteboard, where she'd mapped her client delivery system. Oh, the irony: clear processes for client work, yet stubbornly bespoke proposals for her own business.

Her phone buzzed. It was a message from Michael: "Hey, I just used your delegation framework with my senior physio, and it worked a treat. Not that different from the way I'd run a treatment package with a patient, actually."

"How do you mean?"

"Well, I could design unique exercises for every back pain patient. But I've got standard patient pathways – specific exercises, clear progression points. Patients still feel it's personal because their progress is unique."

"But every business is starting from different points."

"So does every patient with back pain. Your leadership framework helped me delegate admin. The same principles would help any business owner step back. The process stays consistent. It's just the implementation that varies."

Sarah stared at her latest proposal and laughed. Oh my, Michael was right. Here she was, six hours into crafting custom solutions when she already had a proven framework for transforming operators into leaders. It was just like the patient pathway. Everybody starts with different pain points but wants the same outcome goals.

Sarah typed "Signature Offer" in a new document. It was time to stop being everyone's business hero and start building something she could sell and deliver more systematically.

The Trap of Expertise

Like many business coaches, Sarah had spent years honing her analytical skills. Her education and ongoing learning had drilled into her a simple truth: every problem had a solution if you looked hard enough. This curse runs deepest in those who've trained or practised the longest to reach the top of their vocation.

However, this puzzle-solving mindset, valuable for bespoke client work, had hindered Sarah's business growth. Each prospect presented a new set of challenges, including the complexities of its industry and the business's unique combination of problems.

It's the **trap of expertise**.

"I see a problem. I want to solve it," Sarah thought, reviewing her latest proposal. "But trying to solve everything means I end up helping no one properly."

The pattern was evident in her current client base. Despite excellent results, she felt burned out from constant customisation. Every client's journey was different, every solution bespoke, and every delivery unique. The qualities that made her an excellent coach, attention to detail, deep analysis, and comprehensive solutions, prevented her from building a sustainable, scalable business.

She wasn't the only 'broke coach' she knew; her energy, enthusiasm, and financial results all had elements of 'broken'. In her networking groups, brilliant people with impressive qualifications ran businesses barely covering costs. Their deep expertise wasn't translating into profits. Meanwhile, others with less experience gained more traction by focusing solely on solving one clear problem, often because that's all they knew how to do. Their limitations had inadvertently become their strengths.

She thought about John, her most successful client. Although he had initially presented five different challenges, they'd focused on just one: stepping out of daily operations to lead his team. That single focus had transformed his business more than tackling all five issues simultaneously.

"I don't have to solve every problem," Sarah realised. "I just need to solve the right one first."

This revelation challenged everything she'd learned professionally:

- The education system rewards complete answers
- Professional training demands forensic analysis and attention to detail
- Expertise drives us to solve every problem we can identify
- ...But scalable business growth requires focused solutions

You can't 'superhero' yourself to predictable profits or customise your way to systemised success. You have to choose: be a one-stop solution shop for a select few clients, diving deep into their complex challenges, or be a focused problem-solver for many. Unfortunately, part of the expertise trap is that those who opt for the deep-dive model don't price their services at the value their expertise delivers.

We've all got a trap of expertise running through our veins. It's like a virus we keep catching. We're the most significant risk to our own goals and our most certain path to an 'own goal', all at the same time.

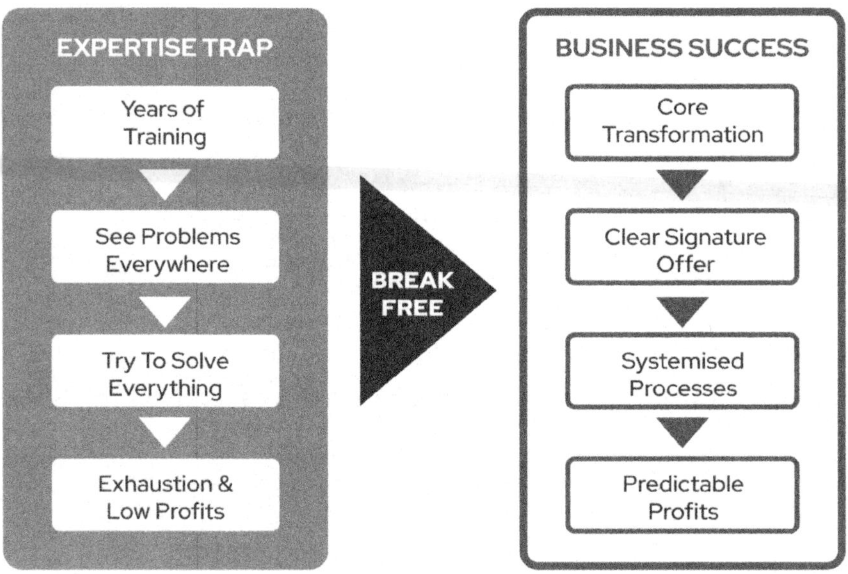

Fig 8.1: ***The Trap of Expertise***

If you feel a burden of responsibility to solve every problem every client has, then you're in the 'Expertise Trap'. It's a cycle of low profits and exhaustion. To break free and find a path to more predictable profits, you need to focus on one core transformation that you can deliver profitably and systematically.

Break Free from Bespoke

Sarah glanced through her recent proposals. In the last month alone, she'd offered to help clients with team development, leadership skills, marketing strategy, financial planning, time management, and business systems. Each proposal showcased her expertise. Each demonstrated a deep understanding of their challenges. Each remained unsold.

She opened her client feedback folder and pulled up her three most successful case studies. Although she could help with multiple areas, each transformation started with the same core challenge: helping business owners step back from daily operations to lead their teams.

Sarah realised that she had been so busy proving she could solve every problem and had lost sight of the one solution she delivered best.

"Eighty per cent of what most of my ideal clients need is the same," she typed into a fresh document. "They need to stop being the business hero and become the business leader."

Those other issues - marketing, finance, systems - mattered, but less than the core transformation from operator to leader. When you get that right first, solving other problems becomes easier.

Sarah started deleting sections from her current proposal template. The detailed analyses of every challenge mentioned and the multiple package options were gone. Instead, she focused on one straightforward journey: helping successful but overwhelmed business owners build teams they could trust to deliver quality work.

"I'm not dropping my expertise," she realised. "I'm applying it where it matters most."

This systematic approach meant:

- One core transformation: from operator to leader
- Standard package delivering the essential 80%
- Clear process every client follows
- Premium support is available after mastering the fundamentals
- Freedom to choose which clients get more hands-on time

By creating a standard program that worked the same way each time, she'd have the time and energy to be selective about clients needing closer attention. Clients who wanted custom solutions could pay extra for them, but only after mastering the fundamentals through her standard programme.

Sarah saw something powerful emerging from this focus. By stepping away from trying to solve every problem, she could create something unique, an offering so specific and transformative that it would stand out from all the generic "business coaching" alternatives in her market. This offering could help her simplify her business and become unmistakably distinctive in the minds of her ideal clients.

Standout Starts Stay Sticky

Sarah discovered a counterintuitive truth about client relationships: the most powerful first step is an offering that makes you a 'category of one' in the prospect's mind and naturally leads to more work. Creating a starter package offer so specific and transformative that it stood out from all the generic alternatives made her initial engagement impossible to ignore.

Her Leadership Accelerator wasn't just another coaching programme. It was a systematic pathway that completely reshaped how practice owners approached leadership. Clients weren't just buying a service; they were investing in a step-by-step plan to change their business.

This '**Standout Starts Stay Sticky**' approach turned her initial offering into a gateway. Clients who experienced her unique methodology trusted her so implicitly that they saw her recommendations as natural next steps, not a sales pitch. Take John's journey. John was the client Sarah had helped to step out of daily operations to lead his team. The structured six-month programme gave his practice a working leadership and team structure that gave them such deep trust in Sarah's guidance that any further work with her would be an obvious next step.

Your Signature Offer

Sarah opened a fresh document and typed "LEADERSHIP ACCELERATOR" at the top. A clear pattern emerged when she looked at her most successful case studies, like John and his growing accountancy practice. Her clients didn't need her to solve every problem in their business. They needed her to solve one problem exceptionally well: stepping out of daily operations to lead their teams.

Her signature programme would focus on:

- Mindset shift from operator to leader
- Team development fundamentals
- Clear delegation frameworks
- Quality control systems
- Progress measurement tools
- Leadership communication skills

The package structure supported this transformation:

- Monthly group training sessions
- Fortnightly implementation calls

- Weekly accountability check-ins
- Clear progress milestones
- Resource library access
- Implementation templates

For the first time, she could see exactly what time and resources each client would need. She would no longer have projects without clear endpoints, add extra work that was not agreed to at the start, or exhaust herself trying to solve every problem at the same time.

"John didn't need my help with marketing until he had a team in place," she realised. Clients could tackle their other business challenges only after becoming effective leaders first. The premium options – advanced leadership development, strategic planning, and team expansion support – come naturally from a place of choice rather than necessity.

Build the complete repeatable package

Sarah sketched her new "Leadership Accelerator" structure on the whiteboard. Gone were the days of lengthy custom proposals. Now, she had clear, consistent packages delivering core transformations.

The programme structure was clear:

- Month 1: Leadership Mindset and Foundations
- Month 2: Delegation and Quality Control
- Month 3: Team Development
- Months 4-6 built naturally on these fundamentals

"This isn't just easier for me," Sarah realised. "It's better for clients too."

Clients would now know what to expect: clear milestones, measurable progress, and defined success markers. If she got those right, she'd be on track for positive endorsements at the end of the programme; reviews, referrals, or repeat work.

This approach had repeatedly worked with clients like John, although they hadn't realised it because of Sarah's previous custom packaging.

Sarah looked at her existing pricing spreadsheet and shook her head. It was a mess of different rates for industries, varied package lengths, and custom quotes – all with inconsistent profit margins. Her new "Leadership Accelerator" deserved better. Regardless of their industry, successful clients shared a common trait: they were successful solo practitioners ready to build their first real team.

She created a simple structure:

- Six-month Leadership Accelerator programme
- A single clear price point and consistent payment terms
- Transparent eligibility criteria
- Clear next steps

It wasn't about being the cheapest but right for the right clients. The price reflected both transformation value and delivery resources. "Clients aren't paying for my time," she realised. "They're paying for a proven path to results."

The clarity brought multiple benefits:

- Faster client decisions
- No more arguing about what's included in the price
- Predictable cash flow
- Easier forecasting
- Knowing how many clients she could help at once

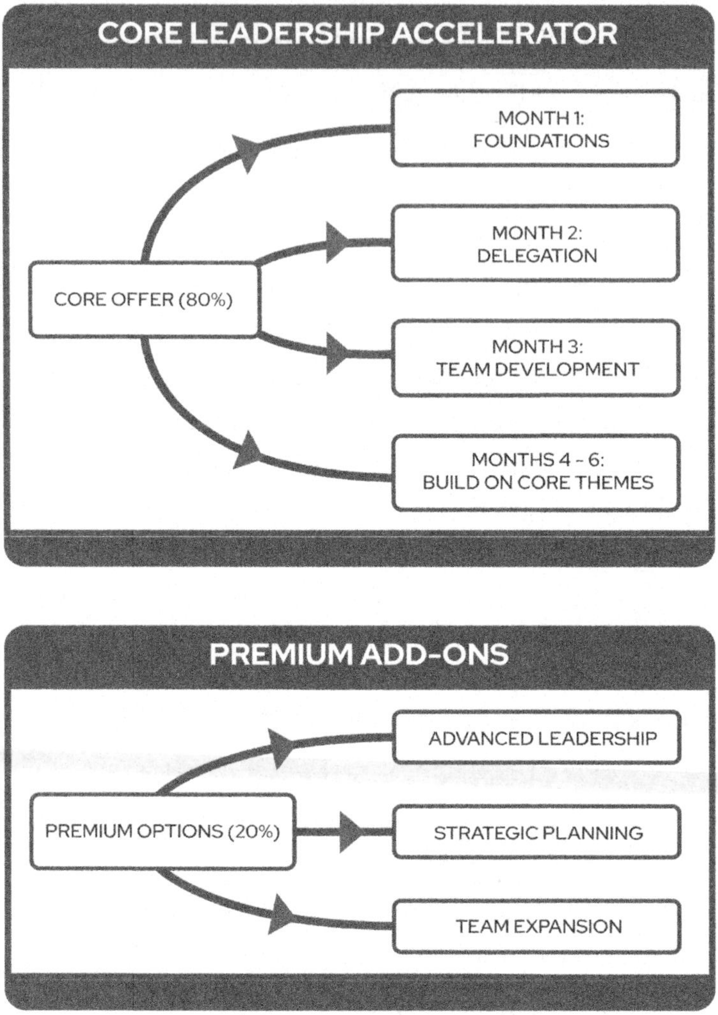

Fig 8.2: ***The 80/20 Offer Structure***

Sarah's core Leadership Accelerator programme delivers the essential 80% transformation that her clients need through a structured programme that starts with the foundations. Premium add-on services provide additional value for clients ready to go further, but only after mastering the fundamentals. The 80/20 model ensures consistent delivery first, with flexibility for deeper engagement later.

For the first time, Sarah could see exactly how many clients she could effectively support each quarter. For clients who later needed more tailored help, she could offer premium services by choice, not necessity. Sarah would no longer need to overcommit because of unclear boundaries or squeeze margins to win work. Instead, she would have clear packages, transparent pricing, and reasonable expectations.

The virtuous cycle

Sarah examined her streamlined business model, seeing a natural cycle emerge that would build momentum over time:

- Her clear "Leadership Accelerator" package enabled consistent delivery
- Consistent delivery created predictable results
- Predictable results generated natural testimonials
- Clear testimonials attracted ideal clients
- More ideal clients strengthened the model

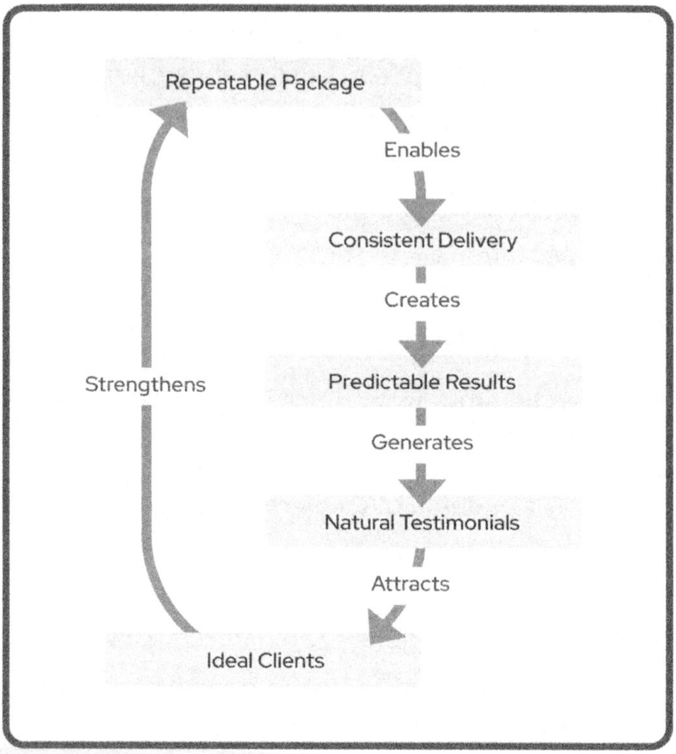

Fig 8.3: ***The Virtuous Cycle of Growth***

A repeatable package enables consistent delivery, which creates predictable results. These results generate natural testimonials that attract ideal clients, strengthening the repeatable package through their success. This cycle builds momentum over time, making growth more systematic and sustainable.

"It's not just a business model," she realised. "It's a success cycle." Each round of clients would refine the system:

- Implementation guides sharpened
- Case studies became more powerful
- Results grew more predictable
- Delivery became more efficient
- Premium options emerged naturally

The contrast with her old approach was striking. Instead of burning energy on bespoke solutions, she could focus on improving one clear pathway and delivering proven results.

Sarah spotted another opportunity: With such a repeatable structure, she could hire associates to deliver parts of the programme. She could even license her "Leadership Accelerator" model to other coaches, creating a new revenue stream.

The possibilities expanded:

- Training associate coaches
- Licensing the programme framework
- Creating train-the-trainer materials
- Building multi-tier delivery models
- Establishing quality standards

It wasn't just about growing her practice. She could also help other coaches avoid the customisation trap by offering them a proven model and creating a new income stream through licensing.

Make it happen

Sarah set aside time over the next two weeks to achieve it. No more getting lost in endless customisation. It was time to focus on building something sustainable:

Week One: Core Package Development

- Document "Leadership Accelerator" journey
- Create session structures and templates
- Design tracking tools and client guides

Week Two: Delivery Systemisation

- Set up group training framework
- Create check-in templates and resource library
- Establish milestones and feedback mechanisms

She'd start with five clients to prove the model, documenting each journey to create case studies and testimonials to attract the next cohort.

Success markers:

- Consistent engagement
- Predictable timelines
- Regular successful results
- Clear measurements
- Natural testimonials

She would offer extra services later. First, Sarah needed to prove this core model worked consistently.

Sarah archived her old proposals folder and felt a weight lift off her mind. The days of late-night proposal writing fuelled by endless cups of tea and chocolate were over. No more solving every problem or exhausting customisation. She'd have just one clear pathway that she would deliver exceptionally well.

"Time to build something that scales," she thought. Her first "Leadership Accelerator" group would start next month, marking her journey from bespoke consultant to systematic business leader.

Building a clear, repeatable signature offer isn't about delivering less – it's about creating more impact by solving the right problem first. As we look at the questions on the next page, let's take time now to plan out your signature offer.

You can't create predictable profits from completely customised work, but once you have a solid foundation, you can add premium services later for those clients who've invested in the right foundations first.

Questions to consider

Scan the QR code to chat with HeyPip AI to get clarity and a tailored plan on this topic in your business.

lemonadeplan.com/ch8

These questions here will help you consider the right core offer for your business. Take a few moments to reflect on your own business, then visit lemonadeplan.com/ch8 or scan the QR code above to chat with HeyPip to refine your core offer:

1. What transformations did your most successful clients achieve first?

2. Which aspects of your service might you be able to standardise for everyone?

3. Thinking about how **'Standout Starts Stay Sticky'**, how might you redesign your entry-point service to be so compelling and uniquely 'you' that it becomes a natural gateway to ongoing work? (It doesn't have to be a premium offer; it could be something lower cost, like this book or an online training course)

4. What steps could you take to simplify your proposals or the method you use to sign up new clients or patients?

5. By solving the one core problem that your market experiences exceptionally well, how might your perfect review differ from the one you identified at the end of Chapter 6?

Like lemonade when the fizz has gone, trying to solve every problem at once can leave you and your clients feeling flat. When work is open-ended or highly bespoke, the work never seems done. To see the impact of the open-ended work problem, compare the number of reviews VAs and freelancers receive to those of carpet cleaners and plumbers.

As Sarah got ready to start her new program, she knew this was just the beginning. In Chapter 9, we'll see how Emma, the virtual assistant, framed her business' 20% 'Add-On' sales opportunities.

Chapter 9:
Natural Add-On Services

> "The aim of marketing is to know and understand the customer so well the product or service fits them and sells itself."
>
> *– Peter Drucker, author and management thinker on leadership, innovation, and organisational effectiveness*

Scene: with Emma, the virtual assistant, in her office

Emma read over her latest client review:

> *"Emma continues to be a great help! She helps us with many different things in our business whenever we're stuck or don't have the time - social media, emails, admin, customer service. Emma is always responsive and willing to take on anything we throw at her. She even copes with our software that we don't really understand ourselves. She can be a real lifesaver!"*

Six months ago, she would have proudly shared this review. Today, it made her wince. "Responsive," "willing," "copes," "lifesaver," every word revealed the problem with her old approach. She'd become the emergency service for overwhelmed business owners, fighting fires wherever they appeared, never solving the underlying problems.

Emma opened her "perfect review" document and read the words she was now working towards:

> *"Emma transformed our client communications from chaos to clockwork. Her systematic approach to managing our inbox, client onboarding, and follow-ups has given us back 15 hours a week and doubled our client satisfaction scores. Best of all, our whole team now knows exactly what's happening with every client at any time. If you're drowning in client admin and losing opportunities through poor follow-up, then Emma's systems implementation, training and VA services are the answer. We're ALL a lot more on top of things now. Worth every penny for the peace of mind alone."*

The contrast was stark. Emma's ideal review showed how her systems helped clients, while the most recent one praised her heroic efforts. She wanted to be known as a transformation specialist who fixed broken systems, not someone who just coped with them for clients.

Her core service package focused entirely on what she did best – transforming chaotic client communications into smooth-running systems. No more frantically jumping between random tasks, no more being the "lifesaver" who kept broken processes limping along.

But something nagged at her as she reviewed her notes. Several clients who used her systems successfully wanted additional help. They'd mastered the basic systems and wanted additional support. The temptation to slip back into "anything you need" mode was strong, yet she knew that path led back to exhaustion.

Emma closed the browser tab for the client review that had made her wince. The networking WhatsApp group had a new message from Michael: "Thanks for that project management app recommendation. But noticed you didn't mention the other three I asked about?"

"Yeah, decided to stick with what I know works. Actually, can I ask you something? Do you treat every type of injury recovery at the clinic?"

"Used to try. Knew enough about most therapies to be dangerous," Michael replied. "Now we focus on backs, necks, knees and shoulders. Tend to refer on anything else."

"Even though you could probably help?"

"Especially then. 'Could probably help' isn't good enough. It's better to be brilliant at four things than average at forty. We send the rest to specialists."

Emma looked at her services list. It was time to stop being the emergency service for overwhelmed business owners. "There has to be a better way to grow these relationships," she thought. It was time to turn random requests into natural add-on services that maintained her quality standards.

Your Zone of Expertise

Emma opened her calendar. Three clients from her 'do everything' days still took up most of her morning. One client alone needed Emma to manage seven different software platforms. No one had connected these systems properly, nor had clear processes. She was just about keeping their business running, but one holiday or sick day would throw everything into chaos.

It was the trap that caught so many VAs: The more capable you become at handling different tasks, the more tasks you are given, until eventually, you are juggling so many balls that true excellence is impossible.

The 'old way' starkly contrasted with her most successful recent client, a business trainer who'd hired her specifically for client communication systems. They used just three platforms (website, marketing, and accounting), all properly integrated, with clear processes that anyone on their team could follow. When Emma took a week off last month, the business ran smoothly without her, which was better for everyone.

"I can't fix everything in their business," she typed into a fresh document. "But I can fix one thing properly."

This realisation challenged everything that the norms of being a VA had coerced her to believe:

- Being endlessly flexible was supposed to be an advantage (it wasn't)
- Saying "yes" to every request was meant to build client loyalty (it didn't)
- Handling multiple systems shows your value (it just exhausts you)
- ...But trying to fix everything meant fixing nothing properly

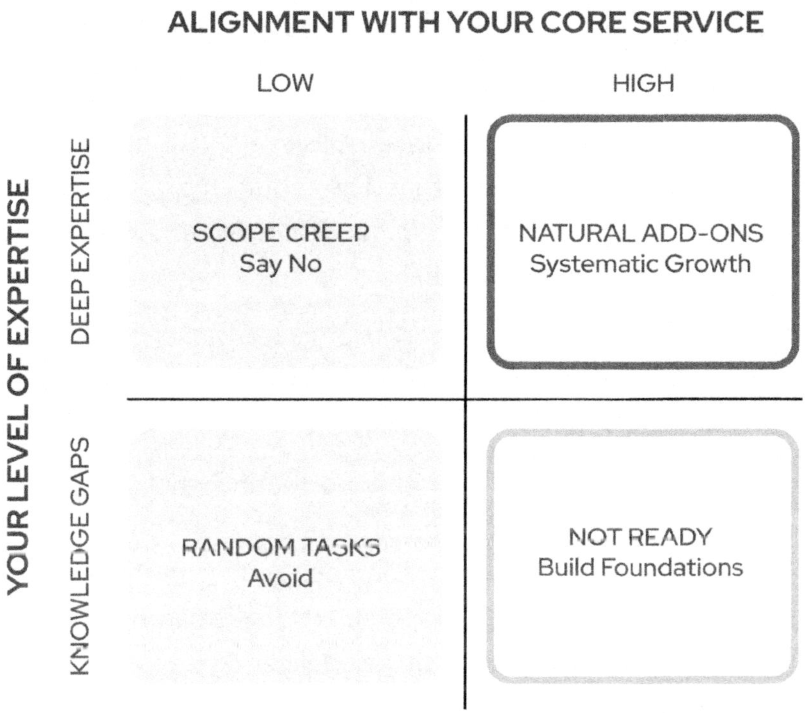

Fig 9.1: ***Your Zone of Expertise vs. Your Clients' Needs***

This is a decision framework for evaluating potential add-on services based on their alignment with your core services and your level of expertise.

'Natural Add-Ons' (top right) include services that are well-aligned with your core offering and your skillset. For Emma's VA service, this was advanced automation and team training. This is your natural option to offer as an add-on.

'Scope Creep' (top left) are requests outside your core service. For Emma, this was social media management, a service that was always stressful to manage.

'Not Ready' (bottom right) are services you cannot confidently provide yet but might do in future. For Emma, this was offering more complex integrations.

'Random Tasks' (bottom left) includes emergency support and one-off projects you and Emma would be wiser to avoid.

Don't forget to also consider your client's readiness for these services. If they're not ready, you shouldn't be offering them. Nothing spoils a positive client relationship faster than follow-on work that is a poor fit for one or both of you.

Because you 'can' doesn't mean you 'should'

If you consider your zone of expertise as the bullseye on a dartboard, many experts have skill levels well above their clients on topics outside that core zone. It's tempting for experts to say 'yes' to helping clients with those topics 'because you probably could'.

Doing a client's work just because you're better at it than a client is a fool's errand because every time you say 'yes' to work outside your core expertise:

- You distract yourself from perfecting what you do best (and earning more from that)
- You can't deliver it systematically or scale it
- You can't train others to deliver it consistently
- Most concerningly, you risk delivering less value than you could with your true expertise

This isn't just about capability. It's about systematic delivery. When you work on tasks outside your expertise, you lose time, money, reputation, and, ultimately, client trust.

Stop Saying "Yes" to Everything

Emma glanced at her inbox, now divided into two clear groups. Her legacy clients' endless stream of random requests was in one folder, while her newer, systematic clients - the ones who'd trusted her to implement proper processes - occupied another.

The difference wasn't just in the number of tasks. Last week, Emma spent three hours helping a legacy client post on social media, time that she could have spent implementing a social scheduling system. Meanwhile, her systematic clients saw real transformation: faster replies, clear client communications, and confident team members managing their workflows.

Emma began mapping out what she now knew to be true in her proposal template: success wasn't about handling more tasks. It was about implementing the right systems in the correct order.

Her core package would focus on the foundations:

1. Email management systems
2. Client communication frameworks
3. Team inbox protocols
4. Document organisation
5. Basic automation setup
6. Progress tracking tools

She'd even include the same software platform in her service. It would help standardise the offer, streamline her delivery, and make the ongoing service revenues 'stickier'.

Once these foundations were solid, natural add-on opportunities would emerge:

- Advanced automation development
- Team training programmes
- Additional software integration
- Process documentation
- System optimisation reviews
- Workflow efficiency audits

The key was timing. Those add-on services would only work once the basic systems were running smoothly. Trying to optimise workflows before basic communication systems were in place was like trying to paint a house whilst still building the walls.

Natural growth paths

Emma studied requests from her recent systems clients. Instead of desperate pleas for random help, she found thoughtful questions about expansion:

"Could we also set up these communication systems for our internal teams?"

"What else could we streamline now that the basic automation is working?"

"Can you train our new starter on these inbox protocols the team loves?"

Each request pointed to a natural add-on opportunity, but only because those clients had mastered the basic systems first. These clients called for strategy sessions, not for emergencies. Instead of asking, "Can you help?" they asked, "What should we improve next?"

She began mapping systematic growth paths:

Fig 9.2: ***Add-On Services Growth Path***

This is Emma's progression from foundation services to optimisation. The **Foundation Phase** establishes the client's core systems, the **Growth Phase** builds on these basics with more advanced services around the same theme, and the **Optimisation Phase** focuses on strategic improvements. Each phase builds naturally on the last, ensuring consistent quality and client success.

Create building blocks step by step

Emma mapped out how these add-on services would work, resisting her old urge to offer everything at once. Instead, she created three clear workflows:

Initial Assessment:

- Review how things work (or not) now
- Check what the team can do
- Find what's missing or not working
- Priority setting

Implementation Path:

- Set up foundational systems
- Schedule team training
- Track progress milestones
- Measure success markers

Natural Progression:

- Plan regular review points
- Find ways to grow
- Check for readiness for add-on services
- Plan service expansion, if appropriate

Tomorrow's client calls would be her first test. Two clients had mastered their basic systems and wanted more support. Instead of automatically saying 'yes,' she could now run checks to see if they were ready for more help:

- Basic systems running smoothly (3+ months)
- The team follows established protocols
- Clear ROI from the current implementation
- Strategic growth plans in place
- Resource capacity for expansion

"This isn't just about selling more services," she noted. "It's about implementing them when they'll deliver the most value."

Keep the relationship fizz

Emma glanced at her whiteboard where she'd mapped out her client delivery system. Her core services worked well now, but as she sketched in potential add-on services, she spotted potential steps where momentum might drop.

"We can't let the fizz escape just because we're expanding," she smiled. Her recent success came from maintaining energy throughout the client journey, so she needed to plan each new service just as carefully.

She mapped the critical connection points:

Planning Transition From Core Service to Add-Ons:

- Progress review meetings
- System health checks
- Growth planning sessions
- Team feedback reviews

Integrating Add-Ons Into Core Service for Clients:

- Clear handover processes
- Success measurement tools
- Quality control checks
- Regular progress updates

The important part was keeping clients excited as they moved to new services. One gap between services could spoil the whole experience.

Emma started documenting where these transitions worked best:

- After successful project milestones
- During scheduled review sessions

- When teams requested additional training
- Following system optimisation checks

The process wasn't about pushing services clients didn't need. It was about being ready for the correct next step when they were ready to take it.

Build your growth engine

Emma typed "Client Growth Path" at the top of a new document. She saw exactly how her business would scale for the first time, not through endless task absorption but through systematic service expansion.

The pattern was clear:

1. Start with rock-solid foundations
2. Build trust through systematic delivery
3. Identify natural growth opportunities
4. Implement add-ons at the right time
5. Maintain quality throughout
6. Say 'no' to everything outside the business' core expertise
7. Repeat with confidence

Tomorrow's first appointment would test her resolve, another overwhelmed business owner hoping a VA could "help with everything." Instead of promising the world, she'd focus on communication systems first, getting those running smoothly, building team confidence, and then, when the foundations are solid, helping them grow systematically.

Emma opened her proposal template and replaced a long list of random services with a simple promise:

"Once your core systems run smoothly, we'll explore natural growth opportunities together. Each new service will build on what's working, and we can implement it when you're ready for it to make the most impact."

That perfect review she'd pinned to her monitor no longer felt out of reach. She was building a clear path forward by focusing on one thing exceptionally well first and then growing systematically.

> Trying to offer too many services dilutes your impact. Start with a core offering that delivers real value, then grow systematically when the time is right.

Questions to consider

Take a few moments to reflect on your own business's growth opportunities:

Scan the QR code to chat with HeyPip AI to get clarity and a tailored plan on this topic in your business.

lemonadeplan.com/ch9

1. If there isn't a clear division between your 'first projects' and 'add-on' projects, do you find client momentum tails off or that you struggle to find the right opportunity to ask for reviews or referrals?

2. In the past few months, which client requests fell outside your core service?

3. Could any become add-on services without losing quality of service, or should they remain firmly in the 'do not do' zone?

Remember: Your best add-on services won't come from saying "yes" to everything. They'll emerge naturally from doing your core service exceptionally well and understanding when clients are ready for more.

Part 5: Build Your Sales Pipeline

Chapter 10: Lead Capture Processes

"A lead a day keeps the downturns away"

– Gareth Everson, systems thinker and author of a book with a citrus drink theme

Scene: with James, the heating engineer, at his desk

James closed his CRM dashboard with a satisfied smile. Last month's Thompson installation had generated another referral. His new delivery process was working beautifully. Tom, his second engineer, completed three jobs this week, following the new process perfectly.

When he opened his inbox, that satisfaction faded. Among the twenty enquiries, he spotted a familiar pattern: "Cheap boiler quote needed," "These guys can do it cheaper... Can you match their price?" Each would require the same time to assess, quote, and follow up, yet experience told him they'd likely choose the lowest bidder, regardless of quality or process.

"We've got the delivery systems in place. Clear packages, job management processes, and proper follow-up. So why do time-waster enquiries still bombard me?"

He frowned at the paradox. After months of perfecting his delivery and creating clear service packages, he'd solved the quality problem but created a new one. Though referrals brought better-fit clients, his website and ads drew in anyone needing heating work.

He looked at two numbers: web visitors and new leads, and the difference told a concerning story. His website had decent traffic, but most left without enquiring. Those who did often wanted something completely different from his carefully structured service packages.

"I've built systems around my delivery," James realised, "but my lead generation is still completely random."

His phone rang. Sarah was calling. " I just saw your new Google review, the Thompsons. Congrats! The new process is working well!"

"Yeah, referrals are great. Just wish I could stop these price-shopper enquiries flooding my inbox."

"Funny, I had a similar problem with my leadership coaching. Then realised I was mistaking every enquiry as someone ready to build a team."

"What do you mean?"

"Most business owners who find me aren't ready for my training yet. Some feel overwhelmed, and others are just starting to plan. Only a few are ready to start. Bet it's similar to your business?"

"Go on..."

"Well, think about the market. Utility bills are sky-high. There'll be those wanting to understand running costs or others wanting to know what radiators work best. Only a few will be ready for quotes. Different stages, different information needed."

"I hadn't considered that. I've just got 'Request A Quote' all over my site." James realised, "Wow, thanks Sarah. How did I miss that?"

"Happens to us all when we can't see the wood for the trees."

James scribbled "Ideal Client Profile" on his notepad. To attract better-fit clients, he needed to be clear on who he wanted to work with, who he didn't, and where they were in their buying journey.

Positioning: What You Do Versus What You Say You Do

James started to see why his website and ads weren't bringing in the right kind of customers when he looked at his homepage. Every service competed for attention, boiler installations next to maintenance contracts next to emergency repairs. The site design shouted, "We do everything!" when his best work, highest margins, and happiest clients all came from doing one thing exceptionally well: high-quality boiler system installations and servicing with clear communication and support.

His recent testimonials proved it. The Thompsons hadn't just praised his technical work but highlighted his approach, clear communication, and thorough handover process. Their neighbours hadn't enquired about emergency repairs – they'd specifically asked for "the same installation package as next door."

Yet his marketing told a different story. "Emergency repairs!" screamed one banner. "Lowest price guarantee!" promised another – a claim left over from his early days that he now regretted. No wonder price-sensitive emergency customers made up most of his enquiries.

James pulled up his last ten completed jobs in his CRM. The pattern was obvious:

Price-driven installations:

- Higher stress
- Lower margins
- Poor communication fit
- Rarely referred others
- Rarely returned for maintenance

Installations from referrals:

- Better margins
- Appreciated his process
- Booked annual maintenance
- Actively referred similar clients
- Followed established communication channels
- Detailed Google Reviews full of praise for the 'little details'

"I'm marketing to everyone," he realised, "which means I'm the ideal choice for no one."

The solution wasn't just about attracting better clients but actively repelling the wrong ones. Every price-shopper enquiry in his inbox stole time he could have spent delivering quality work to clients who valued his organised approach.

Attract vs repel

James looked at his "Ideal Client Profile" document. After fifteen years in the trade, he knew who his business served best, so it was time to get specific about it.

His best clients shared clear characteristics:

- Valued expertise over the lowest price
- Planned home improvements thoughtfully

- Appreciated clear communication
- Understood quality's long-term value
- Followed maintenance recommendations
- Were happy to pay more for a proper job
- Referred others like themselves

He noticed something telling when he looked at his profitable emergency work. Even urgent jobs fell into two distinct categories:

Emergency jobs that fit his business:

- Regular maintenance clients needing urgent help
- Referred by existing customers
- Understood call-out rates
- Followed advice for long-term solutions
- Often converted to maintenance contracts

Emergency jobs that drained resources:

- Shopping purely on price
- Ignored follow-up maintenance advice
- Complained about standard rates
- Wanted temporary fixes
- Never returned for preventive work

"It's not about ruling out emergency work," he typed into his notes. "It's about attracting the right type of emergency client."

The patterns told a story. James realised his website appealed to price-sensitive emergency customers while potentially putting off those who appreciated thorough, well-planned work. The "lowest price guarantee" banner might attract one-off jobs but actively repels those willing to invest in proper solutions and ongoing maintenance.

"Our marketing needs to pre-qualify," he typed. "It should help the wrong clients decide we're not for them before they even enquire."

Content for Where Your Buyers Are in Their Journey

James opened a new browser tab and Googled "new boiler installation near me." The search results showed him something interesting about how different customers searched:

- "Boiler running costs comparison" – Someone researching, not ready to buy
- "Which boiler brand is most reliable?" – Starting to explore options
- "Get boiler installation quote" – Ready to make a decision

The results matched what he saw in his enquiries. Every customer who contacted him was at a different stage in their journey, but his website treated them all the same, pushing everyone straight to a quote request.

Drawing three columns on his notepad, James started mapping out these different stages:

1 – Early Research Stage:

- Learning about heating options
- Comparing running costs
- Exploring efficiency ratings
- Not ready for quotes yet
- Reading general advice

2 – Solution Comparison Stage:

- Comparing specific boilers
- Reading pricing guides and calculators
- Looking at case studies
- Looking at radiators by efficiency
- Requesting buying guides

3 – Ready to Purchase Stage:

- Asking different companies for quotes
- Checking availability
- Reading reviews and guarantees
- Ready for site visits
- Wanting specific prices

As he reviewed his website again, James realised it only served the last group, the ready-to-buy customers. However, Sarah had told him that less than 2% of searchers are ready to buy. The other 98% needed different information, reassurance, and next steps.

He scratched his head. "We're ignoring almost all our potential customers." Just one of his pages, a guide about the right boilers for different house types, attracted visitors for longer, for an average of six minutes. They weren't ready for quotes yet, but they were precisely the type of thorough, research-focused customers who might appreciate his approach.

Three page types, three purposes

"Right then." James opened his website builder. "If we've got three types of visitors, we need three different ways to help them."

He created a new page titled "Choosing Your New Boiler: A Complete Guide." The guide would help those **early researchers** who compare options and costs. No hard sell, just helpful information about:

- How to understand heating requirements
- How to compare energy ratings
- How to calculate running costs
- Answers to common installation questions
- Things to consider around heating system maintenance

Next, he built a "Boiler Installation Guide and Pricing Calculator." Perfect for those **weighing up solutions and suppliers**. This page would include:

- An explanation of the installation process
- Typical project timelines
- Price range guidelines
- Case study examples
- Things that made his process different to other providers

Finally, he updated his "Get a Quote" page for those **getting ready to buy**. But instead of the usual bare form, this page now:

- Set clear expectations
- Explained his quality approach
- Showed example installations
- Featured detailed reviews
- Outlined next steps

"Three main pages, three purposes," he thought, "each matching where people are in their journey." If a page had too much information, he could create additional pages that supported the main topic, but he first needed the three-core page structure.

James had heard references to these buyer's journey concepts elsewhere. Marketing experts use the terms TOFU, MOFU, and BOFU to refer to these stages: Top of Funnel, Middle of Funnel, and Bottom of Funnel.

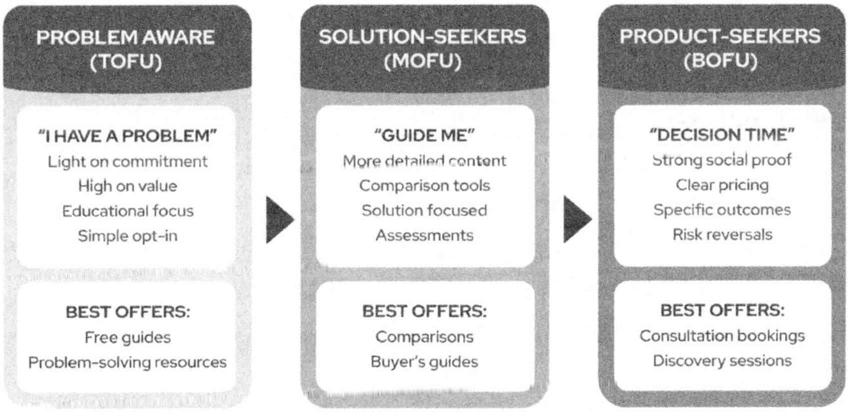

Fig 10.1: ***The 3 Stages in the Buyer's Journey***

This helps you to understand how prospects move through three distinct stages of awareness and decision-making. At each stage (**Problem Aware**, **Solution-Seekers**, **Product-Seekers**), visitors need different content and engagement approaches. When you relate the three stages to where your prospective buyers are at helps you to create appropriate opt-in or sales offers that match where your prospects are in their journey rather than push everyone toward immediate sales conversations (that only a few people want anyway).

James spotted something interesting when he looked at his newly created pages side by side. Each naturally filtered enquiries:

- Researchers could download his 'Boiler Buying Guide'
- Comparison shoppers could use his 'Boiler Budgeting Toolkit'
- Ready buyers could 'Get a Quote'

Better still, each page could lead naturally to the next when visitors were ready - no pressure, no hard sell - just clear next steps for each stage of understanding.

Make Lead Capture Relevant

James clicked through his new website structure. The pages looked good, but something was missing. "It's not enough just to have the right information," he realised. "We need a way to stay in touch with people until they're ready to move forward."

He started mapping out what needed to happen after someone engaged with each page:

For Research Guide Visitors:

- Simple email capture to download the guide
- A short 3-email follow-up series on 'tips about efficiency'
- Add to a smart list to notify if boiler prices change (once or twice per year)
- Seasonal maintenance reminders
- A clear path to comparison tools

For Calculator Users:

- An option for visitors to receive their results by leaving their contact details
- A case study delivered by email

- Installation process guides
- A direct link to request a quote
- Regular updates on availability

For Quote Requests:

- A thorough but simple contact form
- Clear next steps outline
- Automatic booking link for survey
- Deliver their installation guide, explaining the process

"Each step builds trust," he typed into his notes. "But more importantly, each step helps them make better decisions."

James winced when he looked at his current enquiry form. It asked for many details: address, boiler type, and installation preferences. Yet the visitor was new to him and his approach. No wonder many people started filling out the form but gave up halfway through without completing it.

Instead, he created three different contact points:

1. **Guide Download:** Just name and email
2. **Calculator Results:** Name and email in the form, property type, rooms captured in the questions
3. **Quote Request:** Full details once they understand his service

"It's like having three different doors," he thought. "Each one is appropriate to where people are arriving from on their journey."

The real power, however, would come from how these connected the three buyer journey stages. Someone downloading his guide would naturally want the calculator later. Calculator users eventually need quotes, and each step builds on the last, maintaining momentum without pushing too hard.

Transition points between stages in the buyer journey

When James opened his CRM dashboard, he saw how his new lead capture would connect with his delivery systems. The Thompsons' review mentioned feeling "confident every step of the way" – a journey that began months before their quote request when they first researched boiler options.

Each stage needed clear links to what came next:

Early Research:

Boiler guide readers received a sequence of efficiency tips:

→ The tips showcased his installation standards

→ The standards introduced the purpose of maintenance agreements

→ Maintenance benefits appeared in case studies

→ Those case studies led to natural next steps

Solution Comparison:

Calculator users saw real examples:

→ Examples highlighted his process

→ Process details built confidence

→ Confidence created enquiries

→ Enquiries converted naturally

Quote Requests:

Survey bookings followed his system:

→ Installation plans showed clarity

→ Progress tracking reassured clients

→ Results generated reviews

→ Reviews attracted more ideal clients

"Everything connects," James realised. "From first guide download to final review."

Even emergency enquiries would benefit. A homeowner might download his maintenance guide today, use his calculator next month, and remember the value he provided when they eventually need to replace their boiler.

Most importantly, this organised approach to leads would strengthen his existing:

- Quoting process
- Installation standards
- Communication systems
- Follow-up procedures
- Review collection

Instead of pushing everyone to get quotes immediately, he could help them learn about options, compare choices, and make decisions at their own pace. Every step helps clients trust him more and shows how well-organised his business is.

"Time to turn random interest into systematic growth," he thought, opening his website builder. He was ready to create a clear path from website visit to five-star review.

Test for success

James remembered a podcast about landing pages. A landing page is a web page that visitors arrive at first. It focuses on encouraging visitors to leave their details for something valuable. The key message was to start with the essentials and improve based on actual data. With three main pages, he realised he could test and refine each independently.

For his Research Guide, he tried two headlines:

1. "Complete Guide to Boiler Replacement Costs"
2. "How to Choose Your Perfect Boiler System"

After a week, the second headline doubled download rates. People wanted guidance on making the right choice, not just prices.

His "Calculator" page taught him something different. Simplifying it to three essential questions with a "Save Detailed Results" option at the end increased completion rates. People who saved their results were usually a closer match to his ideal client profile.

The "Quote Request" page revealed the most significant insight. Changing from "Get a Quote" to "Book Your Boiler Survey and Consultation" brought better-fit enquiries and set the right expectations about his approach.

"Three pages, three chances to get it right," he thought. He could methodically test tweaks to pages:

- Change headlines
- Adjust form fields
- Test different offers
- Modify follow-up emails
- Update content focus

With only three core pages to manage, each improvement had more impact. Rather than fixing twenty different service pages, James could focus on making these three work perfectly.

Build the bridge to awareness

"Looking good," James thought, reviewing his three landing pages. His lead capture processes were becoming more effective. But staring at his current website traffic numbers, he found something new to worry about. "These capture processes are great, but only if people find us first."

When he opened his marketing folder, his brow furrowed at the mix of emergency boiler repair Google Ads and random local paper insertions. Despite his structured approach to quotes, installations, and lead capture, he only promoted his business when things were quiet.

That's when he noticed something about his competitor's presence. Their vans were always visible in the same neighbourhoods, their social media showed regular installation updates, and their local area marketing maintained consistent targeting. While he was marketing randomly, they were building awareness in a planned and structured way.

It was time to fix that.

In the next chapter, we'll explore how to build awareness of your service. Capturing leads is just the beginning; being where your prospective buyers are looking for help is the next challenge.

Questions to consider

Take a moment to think about your lead capture processes:

Scan the QR code to chat with HeyPip AI to get clarity and a tailored plan on this topic in your business.

lemonadeplan.com/ch10

1. Does your site help ideal clients at the stage they're at? Or are you inadvertently repelling potential customers? What do you offer at each stage of your buyer's journey?

- Early research (TOFU):

- Solution comparison (MOFU):

- Ready to buy (BOFU):

2. Examine your contact forms and lead capture points.

- Can visitors always leave their contact information to get helpful resources based on where they are in their journey?
- Are you asking for too much information too soon?

Remember: like lemonade, leads lose fizz if neglected. Engage your leads at the right stage with appropriate information. Ensure your marketing matches your service quality. It should be organised, clear, and focused on ideal clients.

Chapter 11: Lead Awareness Processes

"Content builds relationships. Relationships build trust. Trust drives revenue."

– *Indra Nooyi, former CEO of PepsiCo*

Scene: with Michael, the physiotherapist, at home, checking social media

Michael scrolled through Instagram, studying his latest posts. Last week's 'Understanding Back Pain' content – which he'd spent three evenings perfecting – sat there with barely any engagement. Meanwhile, his rushed "5 Quick Desk Stretches" from yesterday, hastily posted between patients, had earned just two likes. It seemed to Michael that the physiotherapy clinic across town received constant likes and comments on their explainer videos and patient success stories.

"How on earth do they find the time?" he wondered. At least a couple of times a week, they shared great content - recovery tips, exercise demonstrations, patient transformations - while his feed swung between meticulously planned posts that somehow missed the mark and hurried updates that felt rather desperate.

Michael noticed Emma's latest post celebrating a client's

successful launch event. She'd been sharing the journey over several weeks, naturally building anticipation. There was nothing fancy, just regular updates that kept followers engaged.

"Time to ask an expert," he thought, opening WhatsApp.

"Hi Emma – quick question. Your social content always looks so organised. Any tips? I have a competitor whose feed is full of great content and engagement. I either spend hours crafting posts nobody sees or rush something out when I remember. They must have a whole marketing team..."

"Funny you ask," Emma replied. "I've just helped James to focus his marketing. He was trying to be everywhere and not getting traction anywhere, but now he's almost unmissable in three key postcodes in town. It sounds like you need something similar online. Do you have time for a call?"

"Sure – I'm between patients right now."

How to Become a Market Authority

Michael stared at his Instagram profile. If he were honest, scrolling through his feed felt precisely like his early attempts at local marketing: scattergun and forgettable.

"OK," Emma messaged. "You know where James went wrong at first? He tried to be everywhere, offering every heating service across twenty different neighbourhoods. Now, he's becoming known as the trusted expert in just three areas that value quality work. You need to focus your social media the same way."

"But don't I need lots of different content to attract people?"

"That's also what James thought about his marketing. More areas meant more chances, right? But trying to do too many different things in too many places means you never build real authority anywhere. Look at your competition – they're not trying to be the physio for everyone. They own that space around running and cycling injuries. Every post, every story, every tip reinforces their expertise there."

When Michael examined his content through this lens, he saw the problem. His posts randomly alternated between topics such as back pain, neck strain, sports injuries, and general health tips. While each topic was valuable, none of his posts showed him as the expert for any specific group.

Emma helped him map out what market authority looked like:

- Clear positioning around specific problems
- Consistent presence where ideal clients gather
- Regular valuable insights that showcase expertise
- Natural engagement with the right audience
- Case studies and short quote snippets taken from relevant online reviews
- Growing recognition as the go-to expert

"It's like what James discovered," Emma explained. "When people constantly see him in just three neighbourhoods, he gets better clients than spreading himself too thinly in twenty. You need to stop trying to be everywhere doing everything and start being unmissable in specific places on specific topics."

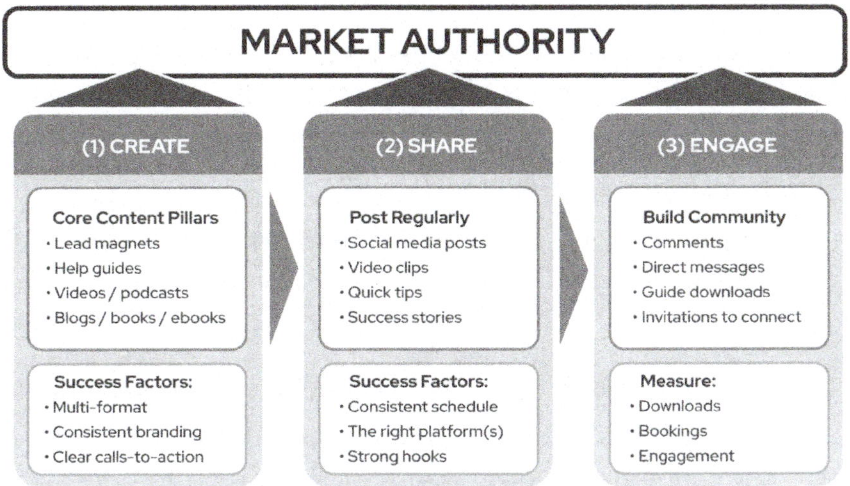

Fig 11.1: ***The Market Authority Method***

When you create meaningful **pillar content** in accessible and reusable formats around your area of expertise, it can be **shared on social media**, which drives **engagement** and leads to downloads and bookings. It builds authority, attracts your audience to step forward as leads, and creates sustainable growth. You need all the parts working together create market authority. One component in isolation doesn't do enough. Do you have all three working hand-in-hand?

Choose your media format

"Right," Emma typed, "if you plan to build market authority, you need to choose where you'll consistently connect with your audience. And I don't just mean 'Instagram' – I mean how you'll share your expertise naturally."

"What do you mean?"

"Think about your best patient sessions. How do you explain things? My clients all have different ways of sharing their expertise. Sarah wrote a leadership book – that's not for everyone – and takes ages. Another client hosts a brilliant podcast because she's chatty but hates being on camera. One runs monthly online workshops. What feels most natural to you?"

Michael thought about his running injuries clinic. He'd started doing short video assessments, recording his explanations of movement patterns. Patients found them helpful, but he hadn't considered sharing this approach more widely.

"The videos, actually," he replied. "When I show patients what's happening with their movement, they understand it better than if I just explain it."

"Perfect. Remember what we covered in your lead capture setup? You need content that helps people at different stages of their buying journey – those who are just starting to notice pain or discomfort, those comparing solutions, and those ready to book a treatment. Your videos could work brilliantly here."

Emma helped him think it through:

- Quick tips for those just noticing training issues
- Detailed guides for people who are looking for help
- Clear next steps for those ready for treatment
- Success stories showing actual transformations
- Recovery technique demonstrations

"But keep it focused," Emma warned. "Your competitor focuses on helping runners and cyclists, not every type of physiotherapy patient. They're building authority around helping runners and cyclists perform better. Every piece of content supports that journey."

Michael nodded at his screen. He could see how his rushed posts and perfect technical but boring blog had failed. Neither approach showed his real expertise or connected with the athletes he most enjoyed helping.

"Start with those movement assessment videos." Emma

suggested. "They're already working well with your patients. Now, we need to help more runners find them, whatever stage they are in their journey."

Meaningful 'content pillars' not 'passive posts'

"Here's what most people get wrong," Emma typed. "They create passive posts that sit there hoping for attention, instead of building pillars of main topics that help the exact people you want as clients."

Michael glanced at his lengthy 'Understanding Back Pain' post. "I think I might be getting this wrong. Can you explain that a bit more, please?"

"Your competitor's content works because they've built clear pillars around runner problems. What do yours ask you most often?"

Michael thought about his running clinic patients. "Usually things like 'Can I run through this?', 'How do I know if I need treatment?', 'What stretches help?', 'When can I get back to training?'"

"Perfect – those aren't just random questions. They're your content pillars. Each could be a complete guide you break down into regular posts. And look – 'When do I need treatment?' that's perfect for your lead magnet we set up last week."

Emma helped him map out content pillars that would resonate:

- Training modification guides (connecting to his 'Runner's Recovery Guide' download)
- Injury prevention framework (leading to his assessment checklist)
- Return-to-running roadmap (supporting his consultation booking)

- Recovery techniques (building trust through practical value)
- Success stories showing real-life transformations

"And here's the clever bit," Emma continued. "You can present each main topic in different ways. Your 'Return-to-Running Roadmap' could be a downloadable PDF guide, supported by video examples of each stage, quick tip shorts showing key exercises, and even assessment checklists."

"That sounds like a lot of content..."

"Not really – you're just presenting the same expertise in different ways. Think about how you already explain things to patients. Your assessment videos work brilliantly for some, but others prefer written guides they can refer back to. Some want quick tips they can save on their phone. It's not about creating more – it's about making your expertise accessible however people prefer to learn."

Michael thought about his running club patients again. Some studied every detail of their recovery plan, while others just wanted quick reminders between sessions.

"So I could have a 'return-to-running' pillar?"

"Exactly!" Emma smiled. "One proper guide, broken down into video demonstrations, quick tips, and clear checklists. Everything that supports that same journey, but just packaged differently. Much better than random posts hoping something sticks."

Post 'must haves': the hook and call-to-action

"But there's one more thing," Emma added. "Each post needs two key elements – a strong hook at the start and a clear next step at the end."

"You mean like 'click here to book'?" Michael asked.

"Not exactly. Look at your competitor's recent posts. They don't start with 'Here's a running tip.' They open with questions like 'Worried that knee pain means missing your marathon?' or 'Running through pain? Here's how to tell if that's brave or stupid.' They hook attention by speaking to real concerns."

She helped him rework his content approach:

Opening Hooks:

- Specific pain points ("Is your marathon training on hold because of injury?")
- Common fears ("Worried you'll never run pain-free again?")
- Timing triggers ("Planning your first post-injury run?")
- Reality checks ("Running through pain isn't brave, it's risky. Here's why...")

"And for the next steps," Emma continued, "think about where they are in their journey. Someone just noticing knee pain might want your runner's assessment guide. Someone worried about returning to training could need your comeback checklist. Match your call-to-action to their current needs."

Michael thought about his recent posts, which ended with generic "Book now" messages. It's no wonder they didn't resonate. They didn't meet runners where they were in their journey.

"Remember," Emma typed, "every post should open by showing you understand their concerns and close by offering a clear next step that helps. That's how you build authority – by being consistently helpful, not consistently sales-y."

"Think about your running club patients," Emma suggested.

"What do they need to know before a marathon? During training? After a race? That's your content plan – systematically helping them at each stage while building natural paths to your deeper resources."

Build Consistent Presence

"Right," Emma messaged, "now we know what we're creating, let's talk about keeping it consistent. Remember how James maintains visibility in his target neighbourhoods?"

"His vans are always there, even when he's working elsewhere..."

"Exactly. He's visible where it matters, not trying to cover every street in town. Your content needs that same type of presence but online. Better to post twice a week consistently than every day for a week but then disappear for a month."

Michael nodded, thinking about his recent posting spree that fizzled out when he got busy. "But how can you keep posting regularly when you're busy with patients?"

"Block one afternoon each month," Emma explained. "Use that time to create your main content. Look at my client success post you noticed earlier – I didn't write it this morning. It's part of a series I created in one focused session. Four posts, scheduled across the month, each building on the last."

She helped him make a sustainable plan:

- Create one month's content in a single focused session
- Schedule two consistent posts each week
- Set 15 minutes daily for genuine comment responses
- Monitor guide downloads and consultation requests
- Adjust based on what brings quality enquiries

"Here's what that looks like," Emma continued. "Create four

return-to-running posts on your first blocked-out 'content afternoon': one video demonstration, one success story, and two quick tips to use as spin-offs. Schedule them for Tuesday and Thursday mornings when runners are planning their training. When you have quiet moments between patients, use them to respond to comments properly. That helps you build real connections with people."

"And I measure success by...?"

"Don't ignore likes and shares, but look at what counts – leads and bookings. Do more runners download your assessment guide? Are you getting better quality consultation bookings? That's your reputation as an expert growing."

Michael looked at his content plan with fresh eyes. One focused creation session. Two consistent posts per week. Real engagement when possible and meaningful measurement metrics that matter.

"Start with this month's return-to-running content," Emma suggested. Create it in an afternoon, schedule it properly, and track what brings quality enquiries. That's how you build lasting momentum."

"Time to stop marketing randomly," he thought, "and start building awareness in a systems way. Like how we'd work with our patients."

> Just as flat lemonade loses its fizz, random marketing efforts quickly lose their impact. Creating a regular, organised way to reach people means being consistently visible to the right people in the right places with the right message.

Questions to consider:

Generating awareness and leads for your business is one of the most common challenges that makes business owners uncomfortable about running their business.

If that's you, consider the prompter questions below, then head to lemonadeplan.com/ch11 to find inspiration on getting more traction when you share your content and posts.

Before the next chapter on building trust through education, consider where your awareness efforts might have the most impact if organised clearly and repeatedly:

Scan the QR code to chat with HeyPip AI to get clarity and a tailored plan on this topic in your business.

lemonadeplan.com/ch11

1. Think about your target market.

- Which 2-3 neighbourhoods (if you work locally) or online communities (if you're online) generate your best clients?
- How can you become unmissable through a focused, systematic presence there?

2. Which three content topic pillars could you build around your ideal client's most common questions or challenges? Think about what questions they regularly ask (or 'should' ask).

3. Think about ways of sharing your expertise (short or longer-form video, writing, audio, etc.). What format(s) and social / web platform(s) feel most natural to you that you can work on regularly?

4. How could you repurpose your core content into different formats? E.g. videos or podcasts to blog posts, monthly topic themes to webinars

Remember: You can't be everywhere, but you can be unmissable where it matters most.

Chapter 12: Education: Your Greatest Hits Sequence

"Marketing is no longer about the stuff that you make, but about the stories you tell."

– Beth Comstock, former Vice-Chair of General Electric, innovator, change-maker, championed a culture of curiosity

Scene: with Emma, the virtual assistant, at her desk

Emma stared at her CRM dashboard, feeling both proud and frustrated. Her new lead capture system was working beautifully. Last month alone, thirty-two people had downloaded her 'Communication Chaos to Clockwork' guide. However, her pride faded as she looked more closely at the numbers. Only two of the fifty downloads in two months had converted to clients. The other people had simply disappeared, lost in what she now realised was the digital equivalent of her clients' messy inboxes.

"I'm doing what I tell clients not to do." Emma shook her head and opened the follow-up sequence: a welcome email, a basic guide delivery, and then nothing, the exact cliff-drop moment she helped other businesses avoid. Here she was, positioned as a client communication expert yet allowing potential clients to drift away.

The irony stung deeper when she clicked into a recent client's system. She'd helped them build a beautiful nurture sequence for prospects of their interior design business – timely updates, examples of their work, and helpful tips for each season. Their leads remained interested for months and naturally became clients when ready. Yet her leads vanished into the void after that second email.

Emma opened her "perfect review" document and read the words she was working towards:

> *"Emma transformed our client communications from chaos to clockwork. Her systematic approach to managing our inbox, client onboarding, and follow-ups has given us back 15 hours a week and doubled our client satisfaction scores. Best of all, our whole team knows exactly what's happening with every client at any time. If you're drowning in client admin and losing opportunities through poor follow-up, then Emma's systems implementation, training and VA services are the answer. We're ALL a lot more on top of things now. Worth every penny for the peace of mind alone."*

A calendar notification popped up, another client consultation in fifteen minutes. When Emma looked at the prospect's details, she noticed something. They'd downloaded her guide three months ago, and only a chance conversation at a networking event had brought them back into her world.

"How many other perfect-fit clients am I losing?" she wondered as she opened a new document. It was time to practice what she preached and transform her sporadic follow-up into something more structured and successful.

Find Your Email Follow-Up Rhythm

Emma studied her email software, scanning her automation processes. Her follow-up attempts had fallen into two common traps: approaches that, when she saw her clients doing them, she'd termed the 'One Hit Wonder' or the 'Workout Playlist'.

The **'One Hit Wonder'** approach started promisingly: a catchy welcome email, resource delivery, and perhaps a quick "How are you finding it?" follow-up. Then, silence. Like those bands you vaguely remember from one summer hit (Hey Macarena!), it made a brief impression before disappearing completely.

The opposite extreme, the **'Workout Playlist'** approach, proved equally ineffective. For a week straight, she bombarded new subscribers with daily emails, like forcing them through a punishing boot camp session. Tips, techniques, case studies, and offers, she was pumping out content at an exhausting pace until suddenly, nothing. Those who survived the onslaught limped into her monthly newsletter list, losing all their energy and momentum.

What she needed was more like a **'Greatest Hits Album'**, a perfectly curated collection that built lasting fondness with listeners, each track carefully chosen and perfectly paced, delivering value and creating connection.

The longer your relationships with your clients or patients last, the longer those email-nurture relationships must be. This mirror effect creates a natural balance between marketing and sales and the client relationship: patient, supportive, and built on trust and respect.

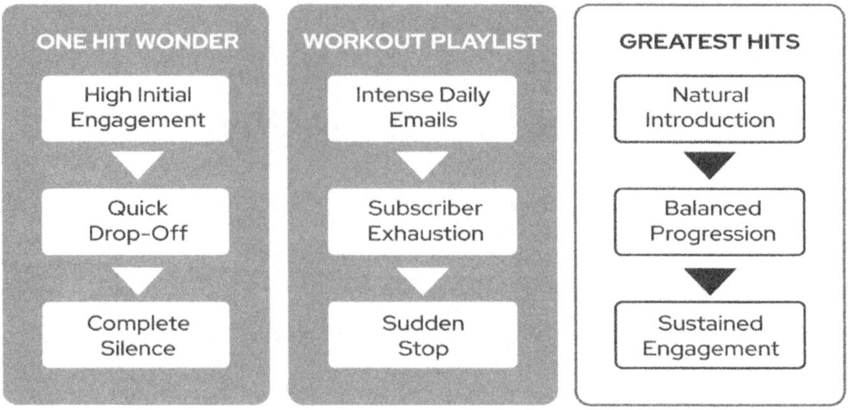

Fig 12.1: ***What's On Your Email Follow-Up Playlist?***

There are three common approaches to follow-up email marketing. The **"One Hit Wonder"** shows the typical follow-up pattern of 1 or 2 emails followed by silence. The **"Workout Playlist"** uses an intensive daily frequency, usually for 5-7 days, that ends in silence and results in recipient exhaustion followed by confusion at no further follow-up. The **"Greatest Hits Album"** perfectly balances well-paced and high quality email content over a longer duration, which builds trust and engagement.

As Emma reflected on her working relationships with clients, she noticed that there was a natural rhythm to the most successful ones:

Early Days (like opening tracks):

Over the first few days, they exchanged quick back-and-forth questions and replies, building confidence. They began to trust Emma, and within two weeks, they worked more closely together and had some initial success stories.

Building Momentum (like the album's core):

As momentum built and clients 'got it', Emma and her clients shared more of their strategic insights with one another. Emma felt it was safe to introduce concepts and stories from other clients' successes.

Strategic Growth (the encore set):

After a few months, Emma would naturally share more advanced strategies and explore ways to build long-term value.

The client implementation rhythm wasn't random timing. Each space allowed for time to:

- Put right what they'd learned in past reviews
- Experience small wins
- Test new things
- Grow in confidence
- Develop relationships

"But if I look at my marketing, I'm treating every download like a ready-to-buy signal," Emma realised, reviewing her numbers. Only two of her last fifty leads were ready to work with her right away, which meant 96% of people needed her to teach them more and earn their trust first.

The pattern was evident in her clients' experiences. Her best clients followed this natural progression, making things better step by step and in an organised way. So why was she dropping her own leads into silence after two introductory emails?

The cobbler's children needed shoes.

She opened her music app and scanned her playlists. Next to her workout mix was 'The Beatles Blue Album, Singles Collection 1967-70'. "Hey Jude," she sang, "Let It Be with these one-hit wonders. Time for an email Revolution."

"We're starting this Magical Mystery Tour," she chuckled as she created a new folder labelled 'Greatest Hits Album'. If she planned to help businesses transform their client communications, she would need to transform her own follow-up first.

"Time to give my follow-up the same planned focus I give my clients' communications," she thought. This focus wasn't just about sending regular emails but building trust, one perfectly-timed message at a time."

Produce Your Greatest Hits Album

Emma opened her guide, 'Communication Chaos to Clockwork', and considered her subscribers' journey. Like any Greatest Hits album, her follow-up sequence needed to balance immediate crowd-pleasers with deeper tracks that built lasting connections.

"If someone's downloaded the guide," she typed, "what do they need next?" The answer lay in her client conversations. Every business that successfully transformed its communication systems followed a similar path: first, quick validation, showing they could make minor improvements. Then, a deeper understanding of challenges followed, followed by gradual implementation. Only then were they ready for strategic growth discussions.

In a fresh document, Emma began mapping out how this natural progression would work in her email sequence:

Early Tracks (Days 1-4):

1. Day 1: Welcome and guide delivery. Set the tone with clear value
2. Day 2: One quick tip they could implement immediately
3. Day 4: Address a common challenge they're likely facing

"This is where most sequences end," she noted. "Just when the real journey's beginning."

Build Momentum (Days 7-20):

4. Day 7: Deeper dive into their specific challenges

5. Day 12: Share small improvements they could implement
6. Day 20: Case study showing simple transformation

Core Value Tracks (Days 33-47):

7. Day 33: Complete framework or audit guide
8. Day 47: Implementation guidance and success markers

Strategic Growth (Days 61-89):

9. Day 61: Show them what's possible once they master the basics
10. Day 75: Address their more significant business challenges
11. Day 89: Guide them toward their next level of growth

The Encore (Day 103 and beyond) – deeper connection:

12. Join our community for support and to answer any questions
13. Share ongoing insights about their industry or problems
14. Share valuable questions that people have

The spacing wasn't random. Like a perfectly curated album, each message needed room to breathe, giving subscribers time to:

- Implement what they'd learned
- Experience small wins
- Build genuine confidence
- Make informed decisions
- Develop real trust

"Every track needs its purpose," Emma typed into her notes. Each email would:

- Deliver immediate value
- Connect to current challenges
- Make readers look forward to the next email
- Lead to logical next steps
- Maintain focus on the main aim

Her education sequence wasn't about selling to readers in every message. It was about building trust until they decided working together was the obvious next step. Just as greatest hits albums curate a band's best work, her sequence would showcase her methodical approach through carefully timed value.

Emma spotted something important in her draft email sequence: like any good album, she needed the perfect mix of content:

Early Messages:

- Focus on helping them implement the guide
- Build confidence through quick wins
- Let them experience success
- There is no sales pressure, just pure value

Trust Building:

- Introduce deeper challenges
- Share transformation stories
- Subtly demonstrate your approach
- Natural invitation to connect

Calls-To-Action:

- After sharing successful case studies
- When introducing advanced strategies
- Where implementation support makes sense
- Together with helpful step-by-step guides
- Through natural conversation points

The key was balance. Too many sales pitches would be like a band playing only new songs at a concert instead of the hits everyone came to sing along to. Too few calls to action would miss natural opportunities to help people ready for more support.

Strategic Content:

- More comprehensive support

- Getting started guides
- Clear pathways forward

"The key," she realised, "isn't just what you send – it's giving people space to absorb and process their thoughts between messages." Each gap in Emma's sequence served a purpose, creating natural momentum that matched how real trust develops.

From first single to sell-out crowds

Emma opened her email software and was ready to set up her new sequence. But something made her pause. Like any new album, this needed testing before full release.

"Start with the basics," she told herself. Instead of trying to write three months of emails all at once, she'd begin by thinking of attention 'hooks' that could open each email in the sequence. Then, when she was happy with that, she drafted the opening sequence – those crucial first messages that would set the tone for everything that followed.

Emma sketched out some rules in her template builder:

Email Subject Line Standards:

- Clear and relevant
- No artificial urgency or misleading promises
- Call out a challenge for the reader
- Under 60 characters
- Intrigue to open the email

Email Guidelines:

- One clear focus per message
- Short, accessible sections
- Start with action steps

- Stories where relevant
- Next steps obvious

When Emma looked at her draft sequence, she spotted another pattern. The best emails, like the best album tracks, followed a clear structure:

- Hook the reader in early
- Deliver immediate value
- Build natural interest
- Guide next actions
- Maintain momentum

Most importantly, she'd watch for those magical moments when subscribers naturally asked for help, ready for deeper conversations about systematic communication improvements. These trust-building signals would tell her more than any other metric:

- Which messages sparked natural conversations
- When people felt ready for more extensive support
- How people used her advice
- Where they needed more help
- What questions kept emerging

"No point having a greatest hits album if I can't tell which tracks are connecting," she thought, setting up her weekly review schedule. She'd focus on what mattered most – building genuine trust through consistently valuable communication.

Emma opened a new guide request that had just arrived and smiled. Instead of feeling pressure to convert them immediately, she could trust her sequence to build the relationship naturally – like a perfectly paced album, each message adding value at just the right moment.

Make it happen: your greatest hits album

Emma blocked out two hours each morning for the next week. Like producing an album, her sequence needed to start with the basics before adding complexity.

She sketched out a simple getting started plan:

Week One: Set Your Foundation

- Choose one lead magnet to focus on
- Create a basic welcome sequence
- Set up simple email delivery
- Test all technical elements
- Check how people react to your first emails

Week Two: Build Content

- Write the first four follow-up emails
- Focus on quick wins
- Include specific success markers (open- and click rates)
- Send emails with a natural spacing between them
- Gather early feedback

Week Three: Extend Your Reach

- Add the following four messages
- Create natural progression
- Include strategic call-to-actions
- Test full sequence flow
- Monitor engagement patterns

"Start small, build gradually," she typed into her notes. Success would come from the same approach she used with clients – one step at a time.

Your greatest hits album email centrepiece

Emma realised something else when she created her Greatest Hits Email Sequence:

- When she introduced new guides for leads to request on her website, she only needed to create new versions of the 'Early Tracks' email group with specific content in those first three emails (Days 1-4) for the new guide.
- All the later emails in the Greatest Hits sequence, from 'Building Momentum' to 'The Encore' (Days 7-103 and beyond), could also be sent to those downloading different guides. All stories, anecdotes and examples in those later emails were relevant.
- This streamlined process created multiple feeder entry points to her Greatest Hits sequence.

The process, known as **'DRY'** (Don't Repeat Yourself) in systems and process design, saved Emma time, reduced mistakes and maintenance headaches, and removed any question marks about what people had read or received.

More importantly, it improved the first experience that early subscribers had with her instead of leaving them feeling empty and forgotten after her old email 'Workout Playlists' or 'One Hit Wonder' follow-up emails to new leads.

Questions to consider

Take a moment to reflect on your follow-up approach:

Scan the QR code to chat with HeyPip AI to get clarity and a tailored plan on this topic in your business.

lemonadeplan.com/ch12

1. Look at your current email sequence(s). Are you a "One Hit Wonder" with just one or two messages, or running a punishing "Workout Playlist" that burns fast and brightly before exhaustion? How could you find a more natural rhythm?

2. Think about leads who went "cold" or disappeared. What information or decision-making tips could you share more of to keep their attention?

3. Which valuable stories or information do you regularly share in sales conversations? To build trust, could you weave these into your education sequence?

Remember: Like flat LEMONADE loses its fizz, sporadic follow-up loses momentum. Your education sequence should build trust step by step by doing these things:

- Well-timed, insightful answers to Frequently Asked Questions your leads have asked before (**FAQs**) – and even better, answers and insights around 'Should Ask Questions' (**SAQs**) that they should be asking themselves and that you would ask if you were in their position, and;
- Once you're confident that they know enough about their situation to be a valuable prospect for you, include subtle calls-to-action (**CTAs**) to invite them to find out more from you or book a call.

The next chapter explores converting interest into meetings once you've built trust naturally. But first, take time to map out your own "Greatest Hits" sequence. Remember: You can't rush trust, but you can build it one email step at a time.

Chapter 13: Meet Better-Fit Prospects

"Innovation is saying no to 1,000 things."

– Steve Jobs, co-founder of Apple, revolutionised design through iconic products like the iPhone, Mac, and iPad

Scene: with Sarah, the business coach, at her desk

Sarah glanced at tomorrow's discovery calls, a flash of frustration crossing her face. Three people had booked meetings: one promising accountant ready to build her team, one seeking general business advice, and one stranger who'd simply clicked her calendar link.

Sarah opened her plan and reread her "perfect review" – transforming solo-owner services businesses into growing firms through her Leadership Accelerator programme. Her recent work on lead generation and education showed promise: an increase in guide downloads and trust built by her email nurture sequence.

As Sarah looked at tomorrow's meetings, something felt off. She'd spent months perfecting her delivery systems and service packages, yet here she was, looking at a calendar full of appointments with people who might not fit her programme.

"I've systemised everything else," she sighed as she clicked into another unknown booking. Why does it still seem like I'm giving anyone and everyone access to my diary?" She opened a new document titled 'Meeting Journey'. It was time to apply the same systems thinking to sales conversations.

The Pre-Qualification Gap

Sarah opened the first discovery call confirmation email for tomorrow. She winced at the automated message, which opened with a generic "Looking forward to speaking" greeting, no agenda, and zero qualification questions, just a calendar invitation and online meeting link.

"Wait a minute," she realised as she opened her Leadership Accelerator nurture sequence. There it was – the same meeting link plastered at the bottom of every message. No context. No qualification. Her social media wasn't any better, with every post ending with "Book a call to learn more!" Even her website had a booking link at the front and centre before people could read about her programme.

Her CRM's reporting told a stark story: 40% of call bookers didn't show up, and of those who did, half weren't ready to build a team. She needed clear readiness markers, like a completed leadership scorecard survey or signs showing the business owner wanted to hire people and grow.

She thought about John, her ideal client. He'd ticked every readiness box – guide implementation, team changes started, and thoughtful questions about the next steps. By contrast, her current system allowed anyone to book time, regardless of preparation. She could redirect those seeking general advice to her educational content, preserving her calendar for transformation-ready prospects.

"I'm training people to expect one-to-one help for everything," she realised. "Why would they engage with my content when they can just book a call?"

Sarah opened her booking system settings. Her phone rang. It was James.

"Quick one – what do I need to prep for that chat about my team planning?"

"Hang on, haven't you booked through my calendar link?"

"Yeah, but thought I'd check first. What do you need from me?"

"What do you mean?"

"Like when someone wants a new boiler. I don't just show up without asking questions anymore – I ask for the basics first. House type, what they've got now. Half the time, they just need our guide about running costs."

Sarah glanced at her calendar. "Like my leadership content..."

"Exactly. I wouldn't put a boiler in without checking it's right. Why start leadership training without knowing they're ready?"

Sarah closed her calendar app and opened her form builder. She was making it too easy to get busy with meaningless meetings. Before anyone saw her diary, it was time to add some qualification steps.

Build a Systemised Meeting Process

Sarah opened a fresh document and typed "Meeting Journey" at the top. Sarah needed to understand each step to systemise her booking process. In the 'Meeting Journey' document, she typed:

Current journey:

Someone finds a booking link

→ picks any available time

→ gets basic confirmation

→ receives reminder

→ the meeting happens (maybe)

She spotted a pattern when she looked at her most successful client conversations – like John's discovery call.

The perfect journey:

The best calls happened when:

→ they'd read about her Leadership Accelerator

→ understood her focus on team building

→ implemented initial suggestions

→ had thoughtful questions about the next steps

→ were ready to discuss transformation

"Right," she concluded and opened her CRM's automation builder. "Time to create different paths for different stages."

She mapped out three distinct journeys:

1. **Early Stage Prospects**: Guide them to educational content first
2. **Solution Researchers:** Proper qualification questions and programme overview
3. **Ready for Change:** Team readiness assessment and investment discussion prep

"It's not about making it harder to book," she realised. "It's about guiding people to the right conversation at the right time."

Conversations that convert

Sarah reflected on her best client meetings. The ones where real transformation began weren't presentations – they were comfortable conversations that revealed what solo owners truly needed.

Sarah reflected on John's first meeting. The preparation process had been thorough. She'd asked him to complete a multi-question online quiz that gave her a picture of his business situation when she reviewed the scorecard of responses. However, the most significant difference in her process was shifting to active listening, absorbing every detail, tone, and unspoken concern, not just waiting for her turn to speak.

"The more I pushed my programme in other meetings, the less I learned about their challenges," she wrote. Instead, she needed to understand their world first:

1. "Tell me about your practice journey so far?"
2. "What made you start thinking about building a team?"

That second question often revealed an early opportunity to redirect. Some weren't ready for her Leadership Accelerator, still seeking general advice rather than actual team development. In the past, she'd have leaned in and helped, showcasing her expertise at a cost to her time and energy. Not anymore. She would guide these advice seekers back to her educational content.

When prospects like John talked about wanting to lead a team, conversations naturally became more meaningful:

3. "What have been the barriers until now that have stopped you?"
4. "How do you see your role changing as the practice grows?"

Each question revealed another piece of John's puzzle: his pride in building a successful practice, his frustration at having to make every decision, and his worry about maintaining quality while growing. Through active listening, she caught his words and subtle signals, the sigh when he mentioned late nights and the energy when discussing growth plans.

When he mentioned staying late checking junior work, she'd asked gently:

5. "What impact is that having on you?"

This question naturally led to discussing how her Leadership Accelerator could help him step into a proper leadership role.

"It's not about selling," Sarah realised, mapping out her new approach. "It's about understanding their challenges deeply enough to know if we can help." When she found the right match, like with John, the conversation flowed naturally to how her programme's systematic approach could support their transformation.

Each question helped Sarah understand whether her systemised approach could transform their business, whether their situation aligned with her offer, and if the prospect was a good fit for her help.

She sketched out her approach:

- Research thoroughly, but keep asking questions
- Open with their story
- Practice active listening – words, tone, and energy
- Ask about impact and aspirations
- Share relevant examples
- Let programme fit emerge naturally

"Every big change," she typed into her notes, "starts with an honest conversation."

Follow-Up Systems

Sarah logged into her CRM to check her follow-up process for discovery calls. She'd overcomplicated eight "checking in" emails where two focused touchpoints would work better.

For conversations showing clear alignment, like John's, she created a simple two-step sequence:

1. 24-hour focused proposal sharing her Leadership Accelerator solution
2. 48-hour reflection note and a screen share recording with key discussion points

For those not ready to start, one clear email redirects them to relevant educational content. There are no generic "just following up" messages – each message Sarah sends has a clear goal. She would document why the opportunity was not right as a way to improve her future pre-qualification.

"How I follow up depends on how well the conversation went," Sarah noted. She provided clear next steps for people ready to change and returned others to her nurture sequence until they were more prepared. This simplified approach resulted in higher conversion rates for qualified prospects and less time spent on misaligned opportunities. Like her delivery systems, her follow-up kept things moving where it mattered most.

Success measurements

Beyond simple numbers like no-show rates and conversion percentages, Sarah needed clear markers to show her new meeting process was working. Sarah mapped her calendar metrics onto one clear dashboard:

Meeting Quality:

- Right-fit prospect ratio (qualified vs total meetings)
- Discovery call show-up rate
- Percentage of prospects she took to the next step

Conversation Depth:

- Proof they've considered my online advice before the meeting
- Leadership readiness signals
- Clear transformation goals identified

Conversion Impact:

- Programme fit assessment score
- Proposal acceptance rate
- Time from meeting to decision

"These aren't just numbers," she noted, "they're signals showing how well I'm matching the right prospects to the right conversations at the right time."

Questions to consider

Think about your recent sales calls and process:

Scan the QR code to chat with HeyPip AI to get clarity and a tailored plan on this topic in your business.

lemonadeplan.com/ch13

1. Think about your last 10 sales calls.

➢ How many of those people were actually ready to buy your main service?

➢ Where did your best leads come from?

2. Look at how people book meetings with you.

➢ Is it too easy for anyone to get on your calendar?

➢ Or is it too hard for your ideal clients to reach you?

➢ What could you ask people before they book to ensure it's worth everyone's time?

3. Think about how you communicate before and after meetings.
   - What could you ask people beforehand to make your conversations more useful?
   - How could you make your follow-up messages work better?

Remember: Just as flat lemonade loses its fizz, meetings with the wrong people drain your energy and enthusiasm. Building systematic qualification and conversion processes ensures that every meeting moves prospects naturally toward the right outcome, whether working with you now or continuing their education journey.

Chapter 14: New Client Success

"The first impression is the last impression."

– Ratan Tata, former Chair of Tata Group, visionary leader and philanthropist

Scene: Michael, the physiotherapist, at home, trying to relax but checking his iPad

Michael clicked another email notification and read another patient question before their first visit. Three new patients had booked appointments for tomorrow, a direct result of his recently improved lead generation and education system. His 'morning back pain' guide was bringing in quality enquiries. His email education 'Greatest Hits' sequence built trust. His consultation calls converted smoothly. His systematic marketing was working beautifully. If only his onboarding worked as well.

And yet the questions kept coming:

"What should I wear?"

"Will I need to get undressed?"

"How long will the session take?"

"What if I can't do the exercises?"

Despite going through his systematic education sequence, each new patient asked slightly different versions of the same questions. He had already answered these same questions dozens of times before, but always manually. Others revealed an uncomfortable truth: they were already starting to doubt themselves before they walked through his door.

Michael opened his "perfect review" document and read the words he was working towards:

"Michael transformed my life – from barely able to walk to confidently active. His planned approach, clear communication, and thorough treatment plan gave me complete confidence every step of the way. Eight months later, I'm pain-free and stronger than ever, loving my first pilates classes. If you're struggling with chronic back pain, Michael is exactly who you need."

He felt frustrated seeing how far his current welcome process was from his goal. A notification popped up, another question. Michael looked at his 'sent items' folder and winced. He'd responded to similar questions dozens of times already this month. Each response took time and was a missed opportunity to maintain the momentum he'd worked so hard to build.

"I've systemised everything else. Why am I still handling this crucial bit – from excited new patient to confident first appointment – completely randomly?"

Michael's phone lit up. A message from Emma: "Your YouTube video about desk posture really helped. Quick question, though – what shoes should I wear for my first session tomorrow?"

"Here we go again!" He laughed and started typing the same response he'd given three times today, then stopped. "Emma, you onboard new clients all the time. How do you handle all their getting-started questions?"

"Funny you ask. Sorry, am I one of 'those' patients? It used to drive me mad, answering the same things slightly differently each time. Then, I had a client miss an important deadline because I'd forgotten to mention something basic. Never again."

"What did you do?"

"Made a document of every question clients asked in their first two weeks. Added my own 'should ask' questions – things they might not think to ask but need to know. Turned it all into a proper welcome guide and just add to it as anything comes up."

"But don't they still ask questions?"

"Some do, but now I send everything two weeks before they start. Give them time to read and really prepare. Works better for everyone – they feel more confident, I don't miss anything important."

Michael looked at his sent items folder. All those patient questions weren't the problem; they were the solution. He needed a welcome guide that turned common concerns into confidence builders.

Avoid the Post-Purchase Plummet

Michael opened his calendar, studying his recent patients' journeys. His discovery consultation calls ended brilliantly – people were excited about starting treatment, confident in his approach, and ready to begin recovery. Yet that momentum evaporated somewhere between the enthusiasm of booking and the first visit.

Michael mapped out the typical journey in his email automation workflows:

During Discovery Call Consultation:

- High energy and engagement
- A clear understanding of the treatment approach
- Excited about starting the recovery
- Confident in their decision
- Ready for transformation

After Booking:

- Basic booking confirmation
- Scattered preparation emails
- Growing anxiety about what to expect
- Wavering confidence
- Lost momentum

"I'm creating these **cliff-drop moments**," he realised. "All that trust built through marketing, all that confidence they gained from the consultation disappears because I don't keep the same momentum and energy after they book."

As Michael examined his recent patients' journeys more deeply, he thought about Jenny, who'd expected to return to running after just two sessions. Like many during discovery calls, people expressed hopes of quick relief: "I just want to play with my grandchildren again" or "I'd love to be playing golf again by next month." That enthusiasm helped them decide to book, but without setting the right expectations, it could leave them feeling disappointed.

The education process or sales consultations should have addressed this gap that creates a risk point between hope and reality.

Michael made some notes for what the patient should expect to commit to recover fully.

Michael's notes: 'What You Need for Recovery':

- To make gradual, ongoing progress
- Stay consistent and committed to the process
- Complete regular exercise
- Be positive to overcome any setbacks along the way
- Participate as an active patient throughout

Michael thought about Sarah, a business coach he'd met at networking, and Emma, the VA who managed the group's communications. They faced similar challenges with clients hoping for instant transformation. All three shared the same opportunity: managing the gap between client expectations and realistic timelines during sales conversations, not after payment.

"The solution isn't just better onboarding," he typed into his notes. "It's setting proper expectations during consultation calls, then maintaining that momentum systematically."

Sarah's Leadership Accelerator clients often expected instant business transformation, and Emma's clients wanted immediate order from chaos. All three businesses shared the same challenge: managing the gap between client expectations and realistic timelines.

Create Your 'First Impressions' System

Michael reviewed Rachel's perfect first appointment experience. She arrived calm and prepared, but only because he happened to catch her pre-appointment call himself, gave thorough guidance, and sent a proper confirmation. This good experience happened by chance, not because of a planned system.

Michael listed out what every new patient should experience after booking. "Right now, we're relying on them to ask questions," he typed. "Instead, we must proactively give them everything they need before they even think to ask."

He started mapping out a systematic welcome journey:

Discovery Call Follow-up: "Thanks so much for choosing to work with us, [name]! I'm thrilled you're taking this step toward recovery. Many of our patients tell us this first email helped them feel confident about starting treatment. Here's exactly what happens next..."

- A warm, personal welcome
- A clear picture of their path ahead
- Simple first steps they can take
- Resources to get them started
- Something to aim for right away

Pre-Visit Confidence Building: "Let me show you around, so you'll feel right at home when you arrive..."

- Photos of where to park and enter
- Introduction to our friendly team
- What to expect in your sessions
- How we'll work together
- What makes our approach different

First Visit Preparation: "Here's how to get the most from your first session..."

- Comfortable clothing suggestions
- An easy way to record your pain or problems
- Easy exercises to try beforehand (if appropriate)
- What we'll cover together
- How we'll measure progress

"Every message should make them feel more confident about starting treatment," Michael noted. "We're not just filling time between booking and beginning – we're building their confidence in their recovery journey."

Michael could already see where this warmer, more systematic approach would make a difference. Instead of letting patients worry about their first visit, he could help them feel supported, prepared, and eager to begin.

"Patients shouldn't have to wait until they arrive at your office to start their path to recovery," he realised. "When they walk in, they should already feel part of their success story."

Early warning systems and implementation

Michael opened his practice management software. Another new patient had cancelled their first visit, the third cancellation this month. Like the others, they'd seemed enthusiastic during discovery, booked confidently, and then gone quiet. By the time his standard reminder went out, they'd already decided not to come.

"We're missing the warning signs," he typed, reviewing recent cancellations for patterns:

Early Warning Signals: "Seeing any of these? Time to reach out with extra support..."

- Welcome pack not opened within 24 hours
- The client hasn't completed the forms after five days
- Sudden silence after initial enthusiasm
- Multiple rescheduling requests
- Delays in responding to preparation guides

These warning signs show when someone starts to doubt themselves. Michael knew what success looked like: patients who consistently opened welcome packs, completed forms before visits, answered questions, caught and addressed early warnings, and maintained client confidence. However, his current system only caught these problems when someone cancelled or didn't show up.

He created simple response triggers:

Rebuilding Confidence: "Let's ensure you're ready to start..."

- Personal check-in call
- Extra support with forms
- Simplified getting started guide
- Clear success stories shared
- Additional preparation help

Timeline Concerns: "Here's what your recovery journey looks like..."

- Share realistic progress maps
- Highlight small win opportunities
- Explain milestone markers
- Celebrate preparation steps
- Reinforce systematic approach

"We can't prevent every cancellation," Michael noted, setting up his implementation sequence. "But we can spot the warning signs early enough to help those who need extra help getting started."

His success markers were simple:

- Clients open welcome packs consistently
- Clients complete forms before visits
- The team shares answers to 'frequently asked questions' (or 'should ask questions') before clients ask
- The team spots and handles warning signs early
- Clients stay confident throughout their journey

"Start small, but start systemising," he typed into his notes. "Better to have three core elements working perfectly than ten working randomly."

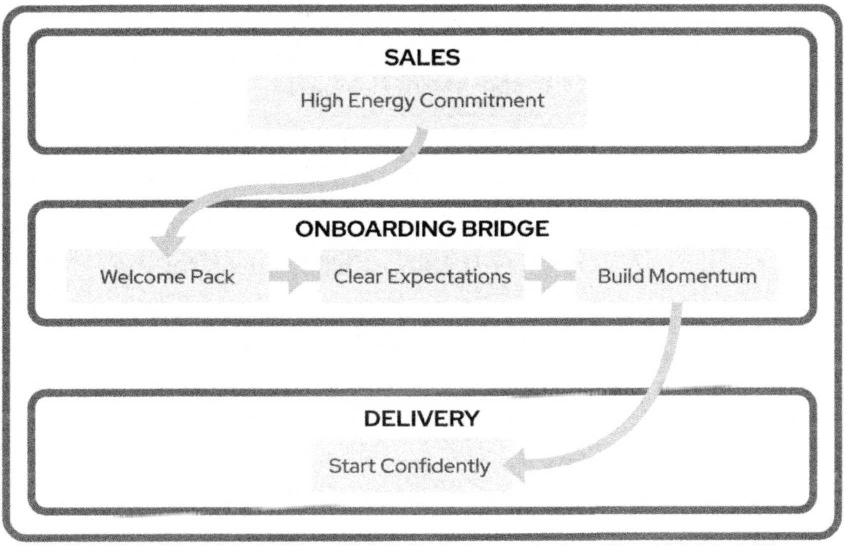

Fig 14.1 ***The Client Onboarding Framework***

This shows how systematic onboarding bridges the critical gap between sales enthusiasm and the start of service delivery. Each stage builds on the last to keep momentum and make sure clients begin their journey with confidence.

"Time to turn first impressions into lasting confidence," he thought, saving his plan. Every patient's journey to recovery would begin the moment they booked, supported by systems that maintained momentum right through to their first visit and beyond.

Questions to consider

Scan the QR code to chat with HeyPip AI to get clarity and a tailored plan on this topic in your business. lemonadeplan.com/ch14

1. Take a moment to reflect on your client onboarding experience:

- What do your clients think will happen after they agree to start?
- What do they receive?
- How long until they see results?
- When does their confidence waver?

2. Consider new clients in the last year.
- What questions regularly come up between booking and starting?
- How could you address these proactively?

3. Where could you turn waiting time into preparation time?
- What small steps could help clients feel progress before they officially start?

4. How well do you manage the gap between expected timelines for you to deliver results with your clients and what those results should be?

- Could you include this in your sales process?
- Think about recent clients who lost momentum. Was it wavering confidence or misaligned expectations?
- How could you prevent this?

Remember: Just as lemonade loses its fizz if left unattended, a client's enthusiasm can fade between booking and beginning. Your onboarding system needs to maintain – or better yet, increase – their confidence when deciding to work with you.

We've explored all eight processes in the LEMONADE Plan, from systematically generating Leads to delivering Endorsements. In Part 6, we'll examine the implementation and see how Sarah, Michael, James, and Emma integrate these processes in ways that make sense for their businesses. Most importantly, we'll help you find your best implementation sequence.

Part 6: Implementation

Chapter 15: How to Make Systems Work

"Vision without execution is hallucination."

– Thomas Edison, prolific inventor with 1000 patents to his name; some great, like the electric light bulb, others bizarre, like an attempt popularise concrete furniture for houses

Scene: with Sarah, the business coach, in her office

L E M O N A D E

Sarah smiled at her laptop screen, scanning the Google search results for "business coach near me". Her business appeared proudly in what Google calls the "3-Pack" – those three local businesses that appear at the top of search results with their maps, reviews, and contact details. Six months ago, she'd barely understood what that meant. Now, here she was, appearing consistently whenever someone in her area searched for business coaching.

In the "Leadership Accelerator" dashboard, the transformation was evident. Sarah's perfect review – the one she'd worked backwards from – was no longer just a goal pinned above her monitor. It was reality, repeated consistently by ideal clients.

She clicked through to her programme delivery metrics. Another cohort progressed smoothly through her leadership development programme. No more trying to solve every business challenge at once. A clear focus should be on that core transformation from operator to leader, delivered systematically every time.

She chuckled that she'd no longer be creating logistics spikes in Tesco's supply chain now that she didn't need the Dairy Milk and HobNobs to get through writing bespoke proposals late into the evenings. She was enjoying having her evenings back again.

When Sarah looked at her old implementation attempts, she had to laugh. Fourteen different apps had promised perfection, and each new app webinar she attended offered another "ultimate solution." On the planning side, every strategy document she drafted was more comprehensive than the last, yet implementation remained stubbornly incomplete.

"I could have handled triple the work if I'd just got out of my own way," she thought, remembering those words to her accountant months ago. Back then, perfect planning had felt like progress. Now she knew better – she succeeded in implementing changes by starting somewhere specific and building systematically.

Sarah began typing in a new document titled 'Implementation Case Study'. Other business owners needed to know that experience (aka 'being older'!) wasn't a barrier to business systemisation, it was an advantage. Experience brings clarity, wisdom, authority, and lots of great stories. And those tech fears? They'd turned out to be much smaller obstacles than her perfectionism.

Perfectionist paralysis had been her barrier to success. In her early attempts, she spent more time researching systems than implementing them. Every app discovery call became a diagnostic deep-dive. While her analysis skills helped clients, they held back her business' progress.

Looking up at her whiteboard, Sarah saw how the eight LEMONADE processes naturally grouped into four core business systems:

1. Her **Attraction** system handled Leads and Education
2. **Sales** managed her Meetings and Offers
3. **Onboarding** covered New Clients and Add-Ons
4. **Delight** ensured consistent Delivery, leading to systematic Endorsements

She appreciated the irony. "My expertise had been stopping me from using my expertise effectively." But that understanding had finally sparked real change. From scattered systems to systematic success. From random reviews to consistent testimonials. From tech overwhelm to simplified solutions.

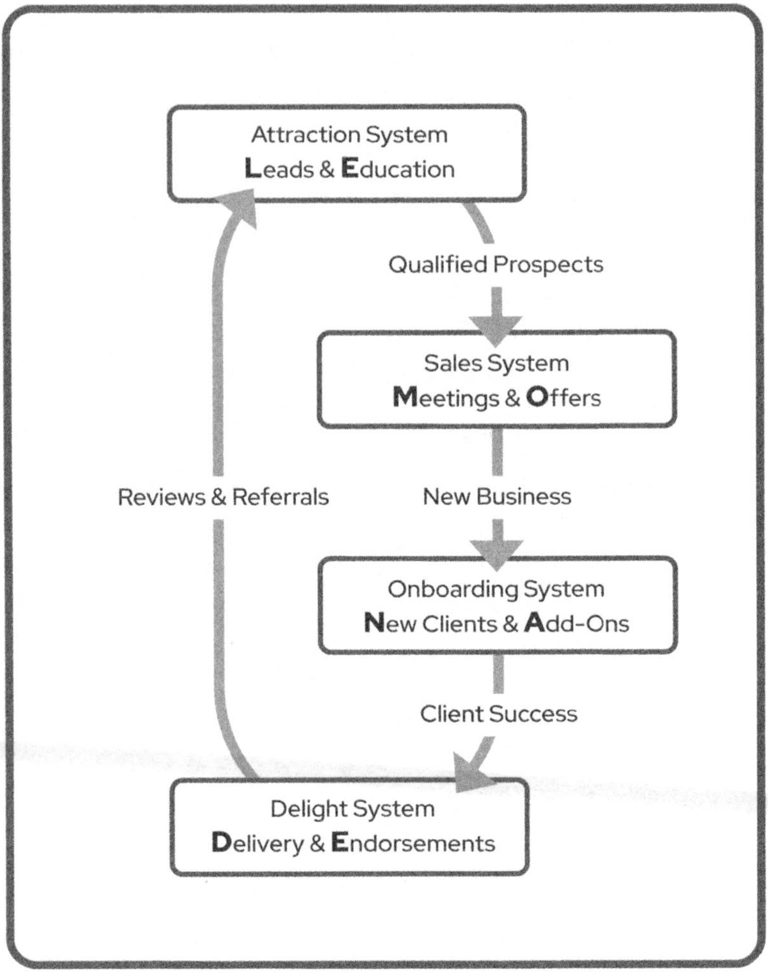

Fig 15.1: ***LEMONADE Plan: Four Systems, Eight Processes***

This shows how LEMONADE's eight processes align with your four core business systems: Attraction, Sales, Onboarding, and Delight. Each system builds naturally on the last, creating a connected path from first contact to lasting advocacy.

The 3 Rules of Systems Implementation

Sarah opened her journal, smiling at the simplicity of her notes from six months ago. Three clear principles had transformed her business from scattered systems to systematic success. The proof was right before her. Whenever someone searches for 'business coaching' in her area, her business now consistently appeared in Google's "3-Pack," those coveted top three local businesses that Google prominently shows at the top of the search listings.

Rule One: Work backwards from success

"The biggest shift wasn't starting with marketing or technology," Sarah noted. "It was getting crystal clear about what she wanted to achieve." That perfect review she'd pinned above her monitor had become more than inspiration – it was her implementation blueprint:

> *"Sarah transformed my accounting practice from a solo operation to a growing firm with three senior staff. Her structured approach helped me become a leader while maintaining quality. Within six months, I had clear growth plans, confident team management, and my first £30,000 month. I'm finally working ON my business, not IN it."*

This clarity transformed everything:

- Each system had to support that core client transformation
- Every process had to maintain consistent quality
- All technology choices focused on scalable delivery

- Success became measurable against clear markers
- Implementation priorities became obvious

The measurable outcomes spoke for themselves:

- Revenue and profit growth
- Planning milestones achieved consistently
- Client satisfaction scores improving monthly
- Implementation timelines met reliably
- System effectiveness measured clearly

"Once you know what success looks like," Sarah realised, "every other decision becomes clearer."

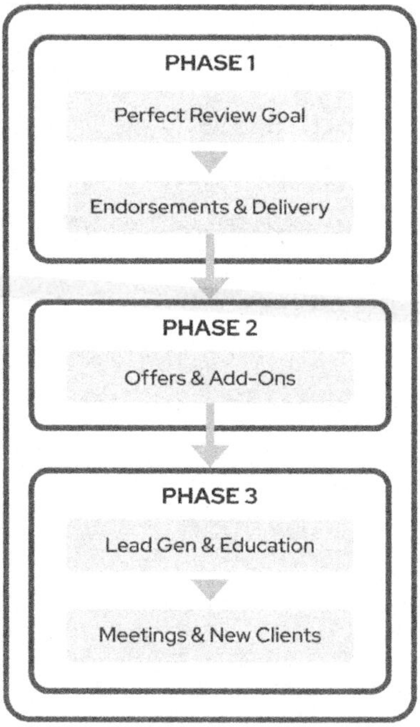

Fig 15.2: ***The 3 Phases of Systems Improvement***

This shows how Sarah worked backwards from her perfect review to systematic success. She first fixed her Endorsement and Delivery processes (Phase 1), then progressed through Offers and Add-Ons (Phase 2) before improving her Lead Generation, Education, Meetings and New Client processes (Phase 3).

Rule Two: Simplification over perfection

Thinking about her old technology setup, Sarah had to laugh. Digital spaghetti had tangled her with apps for almost everything imaginable, yet she'd had no process consistency across anything. She made breakthroughs when she simplified:

- Clear packages rather than endless customisation
- High-quality resources around the one core transformation for clients
- Systematic delivery over constant reinvention
- Natural growth versus forced complexity
- Consolidated operations around four integrated tools, not scattered software

The business impact was immediate:

- Monthly software costs reduced by 33%
- Automation saved her several hours every evening
- Reduced response times to clients
- Got more out of all the resources available to her business

Fourteen scattered tools were now four core platforms that worked together seamlessly:

CRM/Marketing Hub: Managing her "Leadership Accelerator" lead and client journey:

- Client management and nurturing
- Automation and communications
- Progress tracking and booking
- Social media and reviews
- Online community app with resources library for client teams
- Funnel pages, quizzes, scorecards and lead capture forms

Accounting Platform: Handling all financial operations:

- Sales tracking
- Invoicing management
- Payment processing
- Financial reporting

Website Platform: Housing her online presence:

- Blog content
- Lead capture
- Programme information

Video Delivery: Supporting client sessions

- Programme delivery
- Session recordings
- Group training
- Implementation support

Her whiteboard still showed the questions that guided these choices:

- Will it help deliver my core transformation for clients?
- Does it integrate with what's working?
- Can it be delivered systematically?
- Will it scale naturally?
- Does it keep my quality standards?

"The best systems," she noted, "aren't the most complex – they're the ones you'll use consistently."

Rule Three: Integration over isolation

Sarah studied her CRM dashboard and saw how everything now worked together naturally:

Client Journey Integration:

- Enquiries collected on the website
- Nurture sequences get triggered automatically
- Meetings scheduled seamlessly
- Progress tracked consistently
- Reviews requested naturally

Business Integration:

- Revenue measured in real-time
- Planning her available time in advance
- Opportunities spotted transparently
- Referrals growing organically
- Time reclaimed consistently

Each piece of her business now supported the others:

- Clear service package → Consistent delivery → Natural reviews
- Focused marketing → Quality enquiries → Ideal clients
- Systematic processes → Better results → Regular referrals
- Automated basics → More energy → Higher value work

Best of all, proper implementation had created space for what mattered most. Sarah's evenings were no longer consumed by proposal writing. Family dinners became regular occurrences. Weekends meant proper breaks rather than catching up on admin. She had time to plan for the future and to consider business development. She was also a lot more relaxed about her relationship with social media. With more clarity on her offer and market, she could plan posts and network growth around that and break away from posting random stuff just because 'she felt she had to post something'.

"Integrating systems does more than just connect software," Sarah realised. "It's about keeping momentum on every client and reclaiming your life."

Sarah saw how these rules supported each other in her business today. Working backwards provided clarity, simplification made execution possible, and integration maintained momentum. Together, they created a foundation for systematic success.

"Time to help others build on these same rules," she thought, saving her notes. After all, that's what systematic implementation was really about – creating predictable success that could be shared, taught, and scaled.

Sarah's Implementation Journey

Sarah smiled, remembering that overwhelming feeling six months ago. "I'd been overwhelmed by too many how-to guides and systems advice," she reflected. "Everyone was telling me to 'just start somewhere,' but nobody was showing me where that somewhere should be."

Sarah opened her implementation journal and found those early notes from when everything changed. "Looking back now, it's almost funny how clear the path became once I stopped trying to fix everything at once."

Her journal told the story of meaningful transformation:

Week One: Start with reviews

"Everyone said to fix my marketing first," Sarah noted. "But I realised I needed to clarify what I did best." She'd started simply – contacting three successful clients, each running growing accountancy practices and making that crucial shift from operator to leader.

That first email was simple but a breakthrough moment: "Hi John, I've been thinking about your journey from working IN your practice to leading it. Would you be open to sharing your story to help other practice owners see what's possible?"

John's detailed review captured exactly the transformation Sarah delivered best. Two more followed, each reinforcing her core strength in helping successful practitioners become true practice leaders.

Week Two: One clear service

"That was the tipping point," Sarah noted as she looked at those early reviews. "I had five different service packages, but every major success story followed the same path – practitioners becoming true practice leaders."

Her decision felt terrifying at the time – dropping her different types of services spread across too many areas to focus entirely on her six-month Leadership Accelerator programme. "I remember worrying about turning away business," she smiled. "Instead, this clear focus attracted better clients."

Week Three: Natural growth

The focus on leadership transformation as the core offer revealed natural progression opportunities. "Once clients mastered the foundations, they started asking about what came next," Sarah noted. She added new services based on clients' requests rather than her assumptions: strategic planning days, team training workshops, and implementation support.

Month Two: Get the tools right

"I'd been so scared of technology," Sarah laughed, glancing at her now-simplified dashboard. "On reflection, I didn't need fourteen different apps – just four working together properly." She combined her separate tools into one smooth process, supporting every stage of her Leadership Accelerator journey.

Month Three: Marketing with meaning

"Only then did marketing make sense," Sarah reflected. "Instead of trying to reach everyone, I should focus on one clear transformation." Her content showed real leadership journeys. Case studies demonstrated actual results. Each piece built systematic trust with the right prospects.

Sarah looked at next week's calendar and saw four Leadership Accelerator sessions scheduled. Each client will follow a proven path, supported by systematic delivery, and build toward their transformation story.

"That's what real implementation looks like," she noted in her journal. "Not perfection, but steady progress toward one clear goal. Everything else flows from there."

Sarah pulled up the two-page implementation summary she'd created to help other business owners avoid her early struggles. "This is what I wish I'd had when I started," she thought, reviewing the systematic breakdown of each LEMONADE component. From capturing reviews to delivering transformation, it showed exactly how each piece could work together to create sustainable success.

"Time to share your Implementation journey," she smiled, knowing this simple framework could help others transform their businesses just as systematically.

Sarah's LEMONADE Plan Implementation

Here's what Sarah implemented using LEMONADE Plan. The template for this table is here: lemonadeplan.com/resources

Endorsements (E)	
Review Collection System:	Reviews Process Improvements:
• Automated when work finished • 'Share Your Story' email template • 'Tap-to-review' Google review card • LinkedIn recommendation template • Case study permission form • Success metrics tracking sheet	• Review monitoring dashboard • Response templates for all reviews • Local SEO tracking spreadsheet • Testimonial showcase webpage • Case study creation framework • Video testimonial guidelines
Delivery (D)	
'Leadership Accelerator' Structure:	Delivery Processes:
• 6-month transformation framework • Fortnightly 90-min group sessions • Monthly 1:1 implementation calls • Weekly accountability check-ins • WhatsApp support group access • Implementation resource library	• Session delivery templates • Progress tracking spreadsheets • Implementation milestone checklist • Quality assurance framework • Recording management system • Resource sharing workflow
Offer (O)	
Core 'Accelerator' Package Offer:	Proposal Processes:
• £9,000 investment • 6-month structured programme • Clear entry requirements • Defined outcome promises • 6 x £1750/mo payment plan option • Success guarantee terms	• 3-page standard proposal template • Clear transformation roadmap • Investment breakdown page • Getting started guide • Decision-making framework • Next steps workflow
Add-Ons (A)	
Natural Growth Options:	Add-On Sales Process Improvements:
• VIP Day intensive (£3,000) • Team training workshops (£1,500) • Strategy sessions (£2,000) • Extra 1:1 support (£500/session) • Resources library (£97/mo) • Mastermind group (£397/mo)	• Client 'needs analysis' tracking • Client readiness tracking • Track buyer upsell interest signals (email clicks, video watches etc) • Track upsell opportunities on a dedicated sales dashboard

Leads (L)	
Lead Generation Assets:	Lead Capture Processes:
TOFU (Top of Funnel) lead magnets: • "Practice Growth Blueprint" guide • "Growth Blockers Assessment" tool MOFU (Middle of Funnel): • "Systems Audit Checklist" download • "Leadership Style Scorecard" quiz BOFU (Bottom of Funnel): • "Leadership Readiness Quiz" funnel	• Quiz follow-up automation • Guide delivery sequence • Website chatbot flow • Contact form workflow • Resource access system • Automated 'lead scoring' measures
Education (E)	
Greatest Hits Email Sequence:	Education Process Imrpovements:
• Day 1: Deliver lead magnet opt-in • Day 2: In-context to opt-in topic Then combine with Greatest Hits here: • Day 4: Focus on common challenge • Day 7: Success story share • Day 12: Strategic insights • Day 20: Case study showcase • Day 33: Leadership framework • Day 47: Growth strategy guide • Day 61: Team development tips • Day 75: Practice scaling guide • Day 89: Decision support • Day 103+: Regular fortnightly emails	• Fortnightly newsletter process • Content engagement tracking • Sequence performance analytics • Topic effectiveness scoring • Open rate tracking • Click-through monitoring • Content refinement workflow
Meetings (M)	
Discovery Call Process:	Meeting Assets:
• Pre-call qualification form • Automated calendar booking page • Preparation email sequence • 45-minute call structure • Post-call follow-up process	• Call agenda template • Value proposition script • Common objection responses • Investment discussion guide • Templated emails share next steps
New Clients (N)	
New Client Welcome Process:	Onboarding Assets:
• Welcome pack delivery • Implementation guide • Resource access setup • WhatsApp group invitation	• Getting started checklist • First 30 days plan • Tool setup & 'quick win' guides • Success tracking tools

Fig 15.3: ***LEMONADE Plan Implementation Example (Sarah)***

Questions to consider

Take a moment to reflect on your implementation journey:

Scan the QR code to chat with HeyPip AI to get clarity and a tailored plan on this topic in your business.

lemonadeplan.com/ch15

1. Which parts of LEMONADE (or EDOALEMN, if we consider it via the lens of your business systems) feel most urgent for your business?

➢ Where are you losing the most time or opportunities?

2. Consider your years of experience doing what you do.

➢ What do clients repeatedly praise?

➢ Could you systemise any of the ways you've done that?

3. Which of your current processes depend entirely on you? List them in order of how much time they consume.

4. Based on Sarah's experience, which specific assets do you think your business would benefit from first? What content do you already have in different places that you could systemise in a more reusable way?

5. Where does your client journey lose momentum? At what points do opportunities slip away?

Additional implementation stories

While Sarah's journey shows one path to systematic success, every business faces unique challenges. In the online resources at lemonadeplan.com/resources, you'll find your own blank template for the plan and implementation ideas, along with detailed implementation case studies that show the other business owners' plans:

- James (Heating Engineer): Systemised a local service business
- Michael (Physiotherapist): Transformed a healthcare practice
- Emma (Virtual Assistant): Built systematic client communications

Each story offers specific insights for different business types, showing how the LEMONADE processes adapt to various situations.

Download The Blank Template

Scan the QR code to access your blank **template for the LEMONADE Plan** steps and implementation ideas, along with detailed implementation case studies that show all four business owners' plans

lemonadeplan.com/resources

Time to move forward

In Chapter 16: Tools and Support, we'll explore the tools to help you implement these systems in your business. You'll learn how to:

- Choose the right core tools
- Integrate them effectively
- Avoid technology overwhelm
- Build sustainable processes
- Scale systematically

Remember: As Sarah's journey shows, implementation success isn't about having perfect systems – it's about making clear choices based on what matters as a priority for your business.

Chapter 16: Tools and Support

"The best investment is in the tools of one's own trade."

– Benjamin Franklin, inventor and Founding Father of the United States of America

Scene: with Emma, the virtual assistant, at her desk

Emma stared at her dashboard – one clean screen showing everything she needed to manage her growing VA business. She found the subscription tracking spreadsheet from six months ago in her "Implementation" folder. She saw how much had changed:

Before: £525 monthly (13% of her £48,000/yr revenue)

- Chaotic – 12 scattered tools
- Multiple overlapping or unused subscriptions
- Constant app switching
- None of her tools worked together properly (like digital spaghetti!)
- Time wasted on manual tasks

After: £285 monthly (around 7% of revenue)

- More clarity – 1 central platform, 3 core apps in total
- All her tools work together seamlessly
- Clear processes
- Supported systematic delivery of projects
- 46% software cost reduction

Emma unlocked her phone and smiled at the latest WhatsApp conversation with Sarah, Michael, and James. What had started as commiseration over tech overwhelm had become a celebration of simplified success. Each had discovered that growth wasn't about having every possible tool. It was about having the right ones working together correctly.

Scattered to Systematic: The Stories

Sarah: The leadership accelerator journey

Sarah's transformation began with a simple realisation: fourteen different tools were slowing her business down, not helping it. "I was drowning in options," she remembered. Each new app promised to solve one specific problem, but because they didn't connect, they created three new problems.

Here are the 14 tools for Sarah's "before" state:

1. WordPress – Main website (kept)
2. Xero – Accounting and invoicing (kept)
3. Zoom – Video coaching sessions (kept)

And she consolidated the following apps into one **GoHighLevel** subscription:

4. Hootsuite – Social media management
5. Mailchimp – Email marketing
6. HubSpot CRM – Contact management
7. Pipedrive – Sales pipeline tracking
8. Calendly – Appointment scheduling
9. ClickFunnels – Sales funnels and landing pages
10. Kajabi – Course hosting and membership
11. RingCentral – Business phone system
12. Typeform – Client questionnaires
13. SurveyMonkey – Feedback collection
14. Dubsado – Client contracts

She now uses four main tools to run her business:

GoHighLevel (lemonadeplan.com/highlevel) is her central hub:

- Client journey management from the first touch to review
- Automated nurture sequences
- Programme delivery tracking
- Communications in one place (email, text, Instagram and Facebook messaging)
- Business phone system (inbound/outbound phone, SMS and WhatsApp)
- Clear progress measurement
- Quiz and survey funnels with questionnaires and assessments
- Social media posting and management

Xero (lemonadeplan.com/xero) handles all financials:

- Programme direct debit payments taken via GoCardless
- Sales tracking
- Clear metrics
- Automated invoicing
- Performance insights

WordPress (lemonadeplan.com/wordpress) powers her content:

- Educational resources
- Programme information
- Success stories
- Integration with CRM
- Lead capture

Zoom (lemonadeplan.com/zoom) enables delivery:

- Group sessions

- Implementation calls
- Recording management
- Resource sharing
- Team training

The impact has transformed her business:

- No more writing proposals in the evening
- Clear client journey tracking
- Systematic review collection
- Predictable cash flow
- Focused growth

Michael: The physiotherapy practice system

Michael's practice transformation focused on patient experience rather than juggling multiple platforms:

Cliniko (lemonadeplan.com/cliniko) now handles practice core processes:

- Patient booking
- Treatment notes
- Managing appointments
- Payment processing
- Clinical records

GoHighLevel (lemonadeplan.com/highlevel) manages growth:

- Patient education
- Review collection
- Showing up in local Google searches
- Nurture sequences
- Referral tracking
- Social media posts
- Simple website, blog, funnel pages and lead capture

The combination delivers:

- Smooth patient journeys
- Consistent communication
- Growing reviews
- Clear metrics
- Predictable revenue

James: Local service success

James's heating business thrives on simplification:

GoHighLevel (lemonadeplan.com/highlevel) is his growth engine, managing:

- Quote automations
- Client communications
- Review collections
- Local visibility
- Service tracking
- Social media posting and sharing positive reviews
- Website pages devoted to specific services and lead capture

GoCardless (lemonadeplan.com/gocardless) manages payments:

- Maintenance plans
- Recurring billing
- Payment collection
- Clear cashflow
- Professional image

His systemised way of working gives him the following:

- Local search domination
- More maintenance contracts
- Regular reviews
- Clear profitability
- Scalable operations

Emma: Virtual excellence

Emma's VA business improved because she used the same methods she recommended to clients:

ClickUp (lemonadeplan.com/clickup) streamlines projects:

- Project management
- Client collaboration and chat
- Templated projects and tasks
- Time-tracking

GoHighLevel (lemonadeplan.com/highlevel) streamlines processes for both Emma and her clients' businesses as she brought them onto the platform under her own 'agency' to simplify and standardise their processes:

- Client communication
- Automation
- Review collection
- Growth tracking
- Social media scheduling
- Lead magnets and survey funnels

Xero (lemonadeplan.com/xero) handles financials:

- Client billing
- Sales tracking and clear metrics
- Performance insights and growth planning

The impact has been clear:

- Systematic new client onboarding
- Growing client retainers and predictable growth
- Regular referrals
- A clear picture of her capacity

Wrap-Up

In a networking meeting six months ago, our four business owners shared a common challenge: they were all using too many tools that looked professional but just made things more complicated and got in the way of running better businesses. Today, their stories show us four important lessons about systematic business growth:

1 - Work Backwards From Success: Start with your core transformation. Sarah's Leadership Accelerator flourished when she focused on one valuable transformation. Simplified systems improved Michael's patient care. James lifted his Google rankings by focusing on job delivery processes that led to better and more regular reviews. Emma's client communications thrived once she practised what she preached.

2 - Bridge the Critical Transitions: Success comes from keeping things moving forward through key handoffs:

- **From Leads to Education**: nurture systematically, not sporadically
- **From Meetings to Offers**: sell naturally, not desperately
- **From Offers to New Clients**: onboard smoothly, not chaotically
- **From Delivery to Endorsements**: collect reviews systematically, not randomly

3 - Choose Your Version of Hard: Building a systematic business takes work. It might feel hard and uncomfortable for a few months, but this is temporary. Constant firefighting is hard until you run out of energy and give up.

- Sarah chose the "hard" of focused transformation over trying to solve everything
- Michael picked systematic patient journeys over random treatment booking
- James selected consistent quality over scattered quotes
- Emma embraced systematic communication over perpetual availability

Start with tools and processes that support your core transformation. Then, work through what's important at each stage. Slow down first to think, plan and do. Then, you can speed up later as the processes connect. Doing it this way means you'll be more likely to create ways of working that reflect how you want to work.

4 - Keep the Eight Processes Connected: Success isn't about having perfect systems – it's about having the right ones working together from lead generation through to systematic endorsements:

1. **Lead** Generation that attracts ideal clients
2. **Education** that builds proper understanding
3. **Meetings** that convert naturally
4. **Offers** that deliver systematically
5. **New** Client onboarding that maintains momentum
6. **Add-Ons** that grow relationships naturally
7. **Delivery** that creates consistent quality
8. **Endorsements** that fuel sustainable growth

When they look at their businesses today, the transformation shows in metrics like revenue, reviews, recovered free time, and energy. Sarah's evenings are her own again. Michael's practice runs without him when he's away. James appears prominently in local searches without constant promotion. Emma's client communications flow naturally without her constant attention.

Their businesses probably aren't notably different from your business. If this book has shown anything, it's that – once recognised – you can fix any missing steps in how you sell and market your business without just defaulting to thinking that your business only struggles because it doesn't have enough leads or that 'you're terrible at sales'.

Now that you've read this book (thank you), you know where to start making things work for you, not against you. Take advantage of the resources shared in the next section to begin putting steps in place to turn your business into one that consistently achieves predictable profits and systematic endorsements.

Resources and Next Steps

"Knowledge is knowing that tomato is a fruit. Wisdom is knowing not to put it in a fruit salad."

– Brian O'Driscoll, Ireland rugby's most capped player and all-time record try scorer

As you've seen in this book, making things work better starts with clarifying what your customers want and what you need them to do. Once you have that, it comes down to setting the communication steps. Michael faced a problem with his new patient welcome emails. However, he mirrored how he talked to patients in person and answered common questions that regularly arose, reducing concerns and giving his patients confidence.

Where the process doesn't exist in your business, is there a relevant and straightforward process you can copy from a different industry that does that job better? Sarah copied Emma's reviews-driven marketing plan. James copied Michael's 'simplest format possible' approach to quote creation.

It might appear complex to achieve, but you don't have to look far for great examples when you know what processes (hint: 'LEMONADE') to look for. The information and experience are out there when you know where to look for them.

This book makes it easier to understand **'what'** to do. The next step is figuring out **'how'** to do it. That's where the resources that go with this book can help you. Some of the answers to those 'how' questions relate to looking at your business and thinking about what your clients or patients need, other parts relate to writing copy, and other parts relate to using software to manage all this for you. Thankfully, there are many practical resources and step-by-step guides to help you start or continue your systems journey at lemonadeplan.com/resources

Perhaps you remember the **'Standout Starts Stay Sticky'** reference in the 'Offers' chapter? It's a unique starter package that differentiates you from other businesses like yours and turns you into a 'category of one', the only business on the market offering exactly what you do. It's focused and specific and gives your first-time buyer a meaningful early result. It's an offer you should give thought and attention to. And need you ask? I've got a few valuable 'standout starts' for you on that resources page and in my own **Greatest Hits Email Sequence**. See the process in action via the **resources** page above.

I hope this book helps you keep more of the fizz in your client, patient or customer journeys.

Best wishes,

Gareth

PS: Here's my private email if you have questions: garetheverson@heypip.ai

PPS: If we've worked together and you recognise an anonymised version of yourself in a story in this book, shhhh... I won't tell if you don't! I'm glad I could help. Thank you for the inspiration and your support 🙏

PPPS: If this book has inspired you to think differently or take action, the very best way to help others to discover it too would be by **leaving a review** – with or without your favourite Beatles song pun – via this link:

So that others like you can discover this book too, please leave an honest review on Amazon 🙏

lemonadeplan.com/review

There are bonus points and karma if you share a pic of the book on your socials.

About the Author

Gareth Everson is a business-coaching systems strategist with a simple outcome he helps clients reach: **work less, earn more and do more things that bring joy and fulfilment to their week**. He helps service-based businesses turn their inconsistent marketing and weak sales into clear, consistent pipelines.

He teaches simple systems for funnels, emails, follow-ups and automation that save time and attract better-fit clients, sharing strategies and walkthroughs using tools like GoHighLevel, Keap, ActiveCampaign and AI, working with clients across the UK, Ireland, Europe and North America.

His clients describe him as someone who "delivers more than systems expertise," "cuts through jargon," and "creates measurable impact". He hosts the *Zest for Business* podcast and a YouTube channel. See his software, projects and connect here:

garetheverson.com youtube.com/@garetheverson heypip.ai askgareth.com (LinkedIn)

Printed in Great Britain
by Amazon

62718792R00141